Clara

an ex-slave in gold rush Colorado

by Roger Baker

Roger Baker (signature)

Black Hawk Publishing
Central City, Colorado

© 2003 Black Hawk Publishing

Baker, Roger, 1951-

Clara: an ex-slave in gold rush Colorado / by Roger Baker

Includes bibliography and index

ISBN 0-9728917-0-6

1. Brown, Clara, 1800-1885. 2. African Americans—Biography.
3. Women—Biography. 4. Frontier and Pioneer Life—Colorado.
5. Colorado—History.

978.8'00496073'0092 [B]

Published by Black Hawk Publishing, P O Box 125, Central City, CO 80427.
303-582-1294; fax 509-695-8691. Available for credit card purchase online at
www.stores.ebay.com/blackhawkbooks

For trade discounts and other information, contact the publisher at
bhp80427@yahoo.com

Bibliographical citations follow *The Chicago Manual of Style*, 14th ed., rev. (University
of Chicago Press, 1993).

Printed by Johnson Printing, Boulder, Colorado, United States of America

Layout & Design by Interfaces, Inc., Pinecliffe, Colorado, United States of America

Cover Photograph: Clara Brown
Courtesy of Denver Public Library Western History Collection

First edition 10 9 8 7 6 5 4 3 2 1

Dedicated to

Mary Myers

A True Friend

$\mathcal{A}cknowledgements$

Anyone writing a biography of "Aunt" Clara Brown must begin by acknowledging the work of Kathleen Bruyn. Her book on Aunt Clara, published by Pruett Publishing more than thirty years ago, was a valiant if ultimately failed attempt to piece together the little that was then known of Aunt Clara's life into a coherent narrative. She, and Pruett, both deserve our thanks for the effort.

But of more help to a contemporary writer, frankly, are Ms. Bruyn's notes, compiled over her 10 years of research and held by the Denver Public Library's Western History Collection. That same collection holds other manuscripts and documents germane to Aunt Clara's story, along with many hundreds of photographs of the Central City and Colorado that she would have known. Under the able custodianship of Jim Kroll, the WHC is an invaluable resource, and its helpful staff and accessibility reflect also the progressive policies of the City Librarian, Rick Ashton. In the summer of 2003 a new DPL branch, the African-American Research Library, is scheduled to open, which will surely facilitate future studies of Colorado's African-American pioneers.

Tammy L. Martin, of the Oberlin College Archives, was most helpful in researching Clara's connection to that institution. Nancy Niero, of the Fairmount Heritage Foundation, helped solve the mystery of Clara's reburial. And Professor Duane Smith of Ft. Lewis College in Durango, surely the state's pre-eminent mining camp historian, was kind enough to review a draft manuscript and offer suggestions and encouragement, both of which were most welcome.

Though the Central City Opera House Association staff were all busy getting ready for the 2003 premiere of "Gabriel's Daughter, " the opera based on Aunt Clara's story, they were still kind enough to coordinate with me on many endeavors; I need particularly to cite the assistance of Heather Thorwald, Deb Hruby and Deb Morrow in this regard.

In Central City itself, I am grateful to the employees of the Gilpin County Clerk & Recorder's office for so many things over the past year, but for her assistance in searching the old property records, I have to especially recognize Colleen Toth. Most of the heavy lifting in that area was done by local author/historian Alan Granruth, to whom all writers about this area owe a great debt. Alan's generosity and diligence have set a high standard for future research. Alan has also greatly aided the Gilpin County Historical Society in so many ways for so many years; Linda Jones, GCHS President, and Jim Prochaska,

Director, have certainly benefited from his efforts, as I have from theirs, and all that the Society has done. Alan has also contributed mightily to the Foothills Genealogical Society, whose publication, *The Foothills Inquirer*, has provided much useful statistical material.

Another local institution of great value is the Gilpin County Public Library. Larry Grieco has put together a skilled and professional staff, and I appreciate all their work on my behalf. Here, too, I should mention the Kansas State Historical Society, which kindly supplied the Gilpin Library with microfilm copies of that state's African-American newspapers, and Mary Hawkins, with the University of Kansas' Spencer Research Library. And, of course, the Colorado State Historical Society is a treasure trove for anyone working on any aspect of Colorado history.

Speaking of institutions, the Central City newspaper, the *Weekly Register-Call*, certainly ranks as a venerable one. Publisher William C. Russell, Jr., and editor Debra Krause were both very gracious to me over this past year, and I can only wish them both many more years of celebrating (and sometimes making!) local history. And thanks to Kay Cullar for the desk.

I know little enough about writing books, but nothing at all about producing them. Dawn Sorrell, of Interfaces, Inc., in Pinecliffe, Colorado, brought her wonderful creativity to bear on the book's layout; Donna Smith, of Johnson Printing in Boulder, coordinated the final production work. Despite the contributions of all these folks, it should go without saying that any errors in this book are my own alone.

There are two other people who, though not directly connected with this book, are very much responsible for its origin. Jeri Bowles is a good-looking, good-hearted Texan with a special love for Colorado history, and Aunt Clara in particular. A group of Clara's admirers, to whom Jeri was the acknowledged "godmother," approached me nearly a decade ago to write a play on Aunt Clara's life, a play which—though never produced—ultimately was the genesis both for this book and the opera to follow this summer.

It was John Moriarty, then Artistic Director (now *Emeritus*) of the Central City Opera House Association, who saw not just the dramatic, but the operatic, possibilities in Aunt Clara's story, and worked years to bring it to the stage. I wish him, and the opera, *Gabriel's Daughter*, every success. But even if the work never becomes a staple of the operatic repertoire, his dogged persistence in bringing the story to life has been worth it to all of us who love the CCOHA, and Central City itself.

Finally, I need to express my deepest and most heartfelt thanks to my wife, Jeri. Her constant support and encouragement has made all my various endeavors over the past twenty years not only possible, but also somehow more worthwhile.

Chapter 1

A child who would become known throughout Colorado as "Aunt" Clara Brown was born near Fredericksburg, Virginia, on January 1, 1800. Or perhaps it was 1803. And the place of birth may have been Kentucky, or Gallatin, Tennessee. And it might have been in 1805, or '06.

The fact that we have such conflicting accounts about such a significant matter as her birth suggests two of the basic problems in writing about this extraordinary woman. First, however well known and admired she became in later years, descriptions of her early years, especially, are fragmentary and confusing—in fact, often contradictory. Even those accounts supposedly derived from Clara's own recollections, written while she was still alive, are frequently in disagreement.

The second problem is related to—and also partially explains—the first. Clara was born a slave. We should no more expect to find records of her birth today, some two hundred years later, than we would of a white family's purchase of a dining room set, or a saddle horse.

Clara was born into a world in which she was considered a piece of property. And she lived as a slave for the first two-thirds of her life. No doubt in part because of the lack of details, of documentation, of this part of her life, many of the numerous newspaper articles and published profiles of her life quickly pass over this period. That these accounts were, exclusively, written by white men would have added an additional reason to move hastily on to more pleasant subjects, to the respect and acclaim she received in her later years.

The sole book-length biography of Clara written for adults solves this problem by beginning Clara's story with her traveling on a packet boat from St. Louis to Leavenworth, Kansas, in the late 1850's, after she had gained her freedom and left the Kentucky she knew as her home for all her adult life to that point. But writing during the turbulent 1960's, Denver author Kathleen Bruyn felt compelled to make an attempt at portraying Clara's life as a slave woman in flashbacks, dramatizing some of the more compelling known events in that life— and freely inventing others.

However laudatory Bruyn's brave attempt, however, we must recognize its limitations. Not only do we know little of Clara's life during those decades of slavery, we can only hint at the effect this life of abject subservience had upon Clara. Dozens of books have been written, films made and shown, television programs aired to try to examine this shameful time and help us empathize with those suffering under—and often rebelling against—this cruel yoke. Some of these attempts have been more courageous than others, some more successful in conveying the horror. And, to be fair, the system itself—though inherently evil—certainly had gradations of humiliation, of degradation. We have every reason to believe—from Clara's own accounts, and what we know of the practice of slavery in Kentucky (where she spent most of these years in servitude), as opposed to the Deep South—that her treatment was relatively benign.

But this very uncertainty about her birth—and, of course, the subsequent confusion about her age that is reflected in all the accounts of her later life—should serve as a constant reminder to us of her beginnings in slavery. It makes her lifelong quest all the more poignant—and her ultimate triumph all the more satisfying.

The first detailed biographical information on Aunt Clara Brown was provided by James Burrell in a lengthy book entitled *History of Clear Creek and Boulder Valleys, Colorado*. The book was one of three produced about Colorado by a Chicago company, O. L. Baskin & Co., in 1880 and 1881: the history of Denver was first, and the history of the Arkansas Valley followed the Clear Creek and Boulder volume.

In the *Clear Creek* tome, wordy introductory sections are followed by chapters written by local worthies on Gilpin, Clear Creek, Jefferson and Boulder counties. Each of these sections is accompanied by a "biographical department...illustrating in numberless instances the career of truly self-made men...." The sketches were by no means numberless—there were 93 in the Gilpin County section, for example—and with Clara's inclusion were not all of "self-made men."[1]

The author of the Gilpin County chapter was James Burrell; we can assume that he was also the author of the biographical section, as his biographical sketch appears first, though the other entries are in rough alphabetical order. Burrell was somewhat of a renaissance man, and had connections to three of the four counties profiled: originally from Maine, he was a founder of the Griffith Mining District with the Griffith brothers associated with the silver camp of Georgetown, Colorado, in Clear Creek County. His place of business was in Central City, in Gilpin County, where he was Commissioner of the Circuit Court for the First Judicial District, while he made his home in Jefferson County. At the time of Burrell's writing, and for years before, Clara had extensive mining and property holdings throughout Gilpin and Clear Creek counties, so Burrell knew her at least in an official capacity; he is listed as the notary attesting to many of her Gilpin County transactions. And by this time, Clara was a well-recognized figure in Gilpin County, with occasional notices of her comings and goings printed in the local newspaper.

Given his personal knowledge of Clara, it is tempting to take Burrell's pronouncement that "Aunt Clara was born Jan. 1, 1800, near Fredericksburg, Va.,"[2] as definitive. What makes us suspicious is the very precision of the date. It is unlikely that Clara herself knew her exact date of birth; records were rarely kept of slave births, and she was likely separated from her parents in her very early years.

However, Burrell included a specific birth date for the great majority of his subjects, and a month and year for most of the rest. He may well have fabricated a date for Clara simply for the sake of consistency, or as a mark of respect. The generic nature of the date—1/1/00—could merely be an indication that Clara was, at the time of the writing, very elderly indeed.

For whatever reason, though, Burrell's date—though his account would have been widely circulated, and is regularly used by later authors—was contradicted by newspaper articles on Aunt Clara appearing just shortly thereafter. An 1882 article in the *Denver Republican*, for example, said that Clara "was born in Spotsylvania county, Virginia, about seventy-five years ago, as nearly as the computation can be made from the events that occurred about the time of her birth."[3] Among those "events" would have been the War of 1812; Clara recalled later "the outbreak of the war of 1812 well, and was a half-grown girl at that time."[4] The *Republican* estimate would therefore yield a birth date around 1805.

Another article, in the *Rocky Mountain News*, keeps the birthplace but changes the date to 1806.[5] Clara herself did little to clarify the issue, even joking in the Central City paper in 1885 "that as far as she was able to learn, she was then 120 years old."[6] Even worse, in the 1860 census her age is given as 35, which would have placed her birth date in 1825!

The exact location of her birth was equally clouded. The citation in Burrell, again, is precise, but perhaps disingenuously so. Later accounts quoted Clara as saying she was born "away down in Tennessee."[7] Gallatin, Tennessee, is sometimes suggested as the exact spot, though her gravestone in Denver's Riverside Cemetery lists Kentucky as her place of birth.[8]

Even contemporary scholarship is divided on the questions. For example, Dr. Thomas Noel, certainly Colorado's best-known historian, uses Tennessee and 1803 in his short piece on Clara on the City of Denver's website.[9] But Mercedes Buckingham, then Assistant Director of the Colorado Historical Society for Public Service and Access, wrote in the July, 1987 issue of the Society's newsletter that "Clara Brown was born a slave in Spotsylvania County, Virginia, in 1803."[10]

This latter declaration seems likely to be correct. Burrell's January 1, 1800 date simply appears too implausible; a birth date of 1803 would still allow Clara's recollections of the War of 1812 as she described, which later dates might not. And the place was likely Virginia, rather than Kentucky or Tennessee.

Sheer numbers, if nothing else, would argue for a Virginia birthplace. In 1810, for example, Fredericksburg, at the falls of the Rappahannock River, had a population of 2,509, with 900 of that number slaves, and another 349 free blacks. Surrounding Spotsylvania County, being more rural and even more dependent on slave labor, had an even greater population of residents of African descent: there was a total of 4,336 whites, in addition to 6,235 slaves and 116 free blacks.[11]

Kentucky and Tennessee were, by comparison, still sparsely settled lands, part of the Trans-Appalachian West that attracted footloose settlers in search of land much as the Trans-Mississippi West did a half-century later. Both had become states late in the century—Kentucky on June 1, 1792, and Tennessee on June 1, 1796—but as of the turn of the century neither one was extensively settled.

If Clara came from Virginia to Kentucky—the latter a western territory of the former until its statehood in 1792—the trek westward would certainly have prefigured her later journey to Colorado. The Wilderness Road blazed by Daniel Boone in the 1700's had become a virtual highway in the early years of the next century, and the motivations and methods for the settlers who poured through the Appalachians offered an eerie parallel to the later gold rush that would bring Clara to the Rocky Mountains.

> *Unheeding the counsels of the cautious, or the imminent dangers and hardships, these intrepid emigrants pushed eagerly forward to reach the much-talked-of land of promise and certain fortune. There were no roads for wheeled vehicles and thousands of men, women and children, braving incredible privations and perils, moved in successive caravans over narrow trails blazed by the tomahawk—men with trusty flintlock rifles on their shoulders driving stock and leading pack horses; women walking beside them or riding horseback with children in their laps, or in panniers slung over the saddle, and with the older children trudging along on foot. Along with his cattle, horses and household goods the settler also brought his human chattels.*[12]

Clara in later life consistently recalled being owned by an Ambrose Smith in her childhood years, though the details varied according to her memory—or the reporter's accuracy.[13] Burrell, for example, wrote that Clara was "a slave of one Ambrose Smith, who removed with his family and slaves to Russellville, Logan Co., Ky., in 1809."[14]

This would have been a typical pattern, for an east coast farmer to relocate to the newly settled areas across the Appalachians with his entire household, slaves included. "The majority of early migrants from the Chesapeake to Kentucky and Tennessee accompanied masters who left home in search of more lucrative opportunities, took their entire workforce with them, and resumed operations in a new locale."[15]

And in fact there is an Ambrose Smith listed in the Spotsylvania County, Virginia, census of 1810, having in his household nine whites and three slaves. He may have been dividing his time between Kentucky and Virginia during the period, explaining his appearance in the Virginia census; or Clara's recollection of the date could be slightly off. Smith is also named in the Spotsylvania County marriage register, wedding Elizabeth Chandler in 1800.

Further corroborating this account, Logan County (Kentucky) court records show the deed of James A. Smith to Ambrose Smith of 100 acres on Big Muddy Creek, in the Russellville area, on April 3, 1820. So there seems to have

4

been an Ambrose Smith, a slave owner, who moved from the area where Clara recalled being born to the region where she lived most of her adult life, in roughly the correct time period.

Bruyn goes into considerable detail on the family and lifestyle of Ambrose Smith[16] but, typically, the admixture of fact and conjecture is hard to separate. We don't know, for example, if the other two slaves in the 1810 census record were Clara's parents. In fact, to be fair, we don't really know if that is the correct Ambrose Smith. If it is, then that scenario is certainly likely, as Clara would have been too young to be separated from her parents, and she never mentioned brothers or sisters in any of her later recollections.

Such a small holding of slaves was typical in Kentucky at that period; the "greater number" of Kentucky slaveholders owned between one and five slaves.[17] There were no large cotton plantations, as in the Deep South; the median number of slaves held in Kentucky was 10.3 per household, compared to 38.9 in Louisiana, 38.2 in South Carolina and 33 in Mississippi.[18] Tobacco was the principal cash crop, but hemp was also prominent, the hemp being used for cotton bagging and bale rope shipped by riverboat to the cotton markets further south. But most farmland was used for food crops and pasturage for livestock.

This lifestyle of small-scale farming ensured a greater familiarity between the slaveholder and the slave, which often resulted in a more cordial relationship. The intercession of overseers as in the Deep South, with the resultant brutality so often recounted, was unnecessary with such small landholdings. As one writer on the subject put it, the slave experience on a "cotton plantation in Mississippi, where slaves worked in gangs under the watchful eyes of an overseer and drivers, was very different from that on a small hemp-producing farm in Kentucky, where the master personally directed and toiled alongside his hands...."[19]

Again, while Bruyn speculates wildly on Clara's life with the Smiths, we can deduce but little from the known records. We don't know if young Clara was a field hand, or perhaps served as domestic help in the Smith home. The census shows there were young people in the household—a boy and a girl each in their early teens, and a girl younger than 10, along with three girls and a boy between 16 and 20—so Clara may have had playmates of her own age. If Clara's parents were part of the household—which is likely, considering Clara's youth in 1809—they may have passed away during this time.

But as for the most important events of this period—Clara's marriage and the births of her children—there is essential agreement among the later-life biographies. At some point—Burrell puts it "in her eighteenth year"—Clara was married. Burrell and the February 1882, *Republican* agree that there were four children: three daughters, Margaret, Eliza (Eliza Jane) and Paulina (Palina Ann in the *Republican*) and a son, Richard. (Bruyn would later name the husband Richard in her fictionalized account, but no contemporaneous description has this information.) Both sources mention that Paulina and Eliza Jane were twins.

No doubt faith and family were the principal consolations of Clara during this period. Her religious beliefs, which were with her to the end of her life, seem to have been implanted in her at a very early age. Years later, Clara recalled that she "got religion" when she was "nuthin' but a chile."[20] The Russellville area was swept with religious revival in the years of 1819 and 1820, and both black and white participated in the revival services held by a Presbyterian minister and a Methodist pastor in a warehouse there.[21] Perhaps Clara's religious faith was forged in that emotional period. Perhaps it was passed on from her parents; or perhaps the Smith family provided religious education, as many Kentucky slave-holders did.

> *Public opinion was not adverse to the religious train-ing of Negroes, and slaves were given religious instruction on many plantations and farms. Domestic slaves often attended the same services as their masters or mistresses, and on the minute books of many of the churches of Kentucky appear the names of slaves who were faithful and devout members. The churches usually had a gallery for the black people, and if not, then in some cases, certain rear sections were reserved for their use, where they enjoyed the preached gospel in common with the whites.[22]*

However perverted the Christian message may have been in such a seg-regated setting, it undoubtedly provided a source of succor and hope for slaves such as Clara. And while their faith could not be taken from them, their families certainly could.

Clara intimately knew this sort of loss. One of the twins, Paulina Ann, "died at the age of about 8 years."[23] Childhood deaths, due to disease or accident, were not uncommon in the harsh living conditions of pioneer societies, and were visited upon families both black and white.

But a second type of separation was unique to the slave—the breakup of a family due to the sale to another owner of some of the members. The basic barbarity of such a system needs no comment, and the details of the practice can be found in dozens of sources. The specifics of Clara's particular history are best outlined in the *Denver Republican* profile:

> *Margaret was sold to a man named Bednigo Shelton, who lived near Morgantown, Kentucky. She died several years after she went to that place. Richard, after growing to man-hood, was sold so often that his mother could not keep track of him, and finally he was lost sight of... Eliza Jane was sold to a man named James Covington, who lived in Logan county, and in 1852 she left the service of Covington. Whither she went her mother did not then know.[24]*

No mention is made of Clara's husband, but their separation would not have been unexpected. The fragility of slave marriages was recognized at their start; the Reverend London Ferrill, a Virginia-born slave preacher who lived later in Lexington, Kentucky, used to pronounce the couples he married united "until death or distance do you part."[25] Even at this most joyous and sacred of occasions, slave couples were reminded of their dependence on the white man's goodwill.

Burrell wrote, however, that upon "the death of her master, Ambrose Smith, in 1835, she, with her husband and children were sold to different purchasers, and they forever parted." The mere words can convey little of the trauma of such an enforced separation. If we assume a birth date of 1803 for Clara, and a marriage as reported at 18 (thus in 1821), none of her children could have been older than 14. Though slaves were rarely sold, independent of at least one of their parents, before the age of 10, it is probable that this reminiscence is accurate.

For while it was likely that the family would have stayed together on the Smith farm, the death of the master would likely have necessitated the breakup Burrell chronicled. Indeed, "[u]nder the terms of many wills it was frequently necessary for the executors to sell property in order to make proper settlement of the estate involved."[26] Sales such as that of Margaret and Eliza Jane to local residents, or those of nearby towns, would have been a typical outcome. Young Richard's fate may well have been even more dire, however.

By this time, 1835, the practice of slave trading in Kentucky was widely established, if widely condemned. Congress had outlawed the African slave trade in 1808, but the right to buy and sell slaves within the borders of the United States remained. But demand for slave workers, particularly on the large cotton plantations in the Deep South, was unabated. Laborers such as young Richard could bring a high price in the slave markets of Natchez or New Orleans. Such an unhappy end would fit the pattern of frequent sales Burrell mentioned, and almost guarantee that he would be forever lost to his grieving mother.

Though Bruyn called the Smiths "[d]eeply religious,"[27] they nonetheless seem to have been untouched by the growing abolitionist movement. Though J. Winston Coleman noted that in Kentucky during this period "[h]umanitarian feelings and personal attachment of masters for their slaves are reflected in numerous wills, many of which make provisions for the comforts, freedom and happiness of the blacks,"[28] Smith apparently made no such provisions.

In fact, there was at that exact time a widespread movement to emancipate slaves, with an eye toward repatriating them in the struggling African colony of Liberia. In Kentucky, this movement reached fruition in the activities of the Louisville branch of the Kentucky Colonization Society. It "raised $805 in 1832, and during the next year the society succeeded in collecting over eleven hundred dollars for the transportation of freed Negroes to Liberia."[29]

Nor would such a movement have been unknown in Logan County. Coleman related the tale of the Reverend Richard Bibb, of Russellville, who in 1833 "liberated fifty-one of his slaves and gave the thirty-two who were willing to go...$444 for their comforts while on the voyage."[30] Certainly the Smiths— and without question their black slaves—would have known of this dramatic action. No such liberation was forthcoming for Clara and her family, however; they were sold, and separated—seemingly forever.

The pain this loss must have caused Clara can only be imagined. Though by this time she was only in her thirties, she never remarried, never bore more children. The loss of her children was particularly painful for Clara; more than thirty years later, she was reported by an acquaintance to have vowed "they should never have another out of her body to take away."[31] And years later, when she had lost all contact with her children, Clara still never lost hope that some day she could be reunited with them.

Chapter 2

While her family was dispersed, Clara remained in Russellville. She was sold to a George Brown, a hatter. It is from him that Clara took the last name she would use for the remainder of her life. Here at last we are on somewhat firmer ground, for Brown was a well-known merchant in that town.

Kathleen Bruyn, doing research for her 1970 biography of Aunt Clara, took up a lively correspondence with Edward F. Coffman, author of a privately printed history of Russellville and Logan County, Kentucky. Coffman provided a great deal of information and informed conjecture about the Brown family.

Coffman noted, for example, that Brown's was one of the old and established firms in the town of Russellville, dating from at least 1819, and employing between 6 and 15 men.[1] He wrote further that "Brown was a well to do and prosperous man. He may have made hats in his home or possibly in an adjacent house on the lot with his residence. He probably used slave labor."[2]

Coffman put the Brown shop on Fourth Street, just four blocks off the public square, and recalled that he was "said to have made woolen, silk and fur hats."[3] Brown's will declared ownership of just three slaves, so it is likely that the majority of the employees in his hat factory were white workingmen. It is possible that Clara, in her mid-thirties by the time of her sale to Brown, might have been utilized there.

But a more likely possibility is that Clara was used as domestic help for Brown's wife and, to an extent, a nanny for the family's three daughters. The eldest, Mary Prudence Brown was married to Richard T. Higgins in April 1836, just shortly after Clara's arrival in the Brown household. But the younger two remained in the family until their marriages in 1843 (Lucinda) and 1852 (Evaline).

Clara may also have been involved in the care of one of the Brown grandchildren. Lucinda married John Leonard Norton, scion of one of the best Russellville families of the early years, on Valentine's Day, 1843.[4] Tragically, young Norton died September 4th, but Lucinda bore him a son shortly after his death. With the marriage such a brief one, Lucinda might well have moved back home into the comforting arms of her mother—and the middle-aged slave woman who would have been a fixture in the Brown home since her childhood.

With Lucinda's son, and the children of Mary Prudence and, later, Evaline, visiting, the Brown home must have been filled with the noise and bustle of childhood. This must have been a bittersweet period for Clara, coming to love these young people while being constantly reminded of her own children.

We recall, however, that Clara would still have been in some contact, however infrequent, with her daughter Margaret, in Morgantown. And at least until 1852, Eliza Jane lived nearby in Logan County with a family named Covington. Knowing of her daughters' fates must have been simultaneously a comfort and a torment for Clara.

By the mid-1850's, though, Clara had probably lost all contact with her children. There were by this time two other slaves in the Brown household: Absolom and Lucy. The latter was probably older than Clara, or at least longer in the Brown's service. Domestic life was serene and secure, albeit touched with the pangs of loss and the constant bitter reminders of servitude. And however comfortable—Clara years later remembered having "plenty to eat and plenty to wear"[5]—it was still slavery. A quarter-century after her bondage ended, Clara still recalled being beaten, though "not of'en."[6]

Still, Clara's Christian beliefs provided her with the strength to survive. Coffman noted that "[t]he Russellville Baptist and Methodist had Negro members in the 1830s and on. There was a balcony in the old Methodist Church which was used by Negroes."[7]

Clara undoubtedly participated in the religious life of the community. There was at this time in Russellville an elderly black man, known universally as "Uncle" Butler, who preached the gospel to whites and blacks alike. Born in Virginia in 1784, Uncle Butler was taught to read by his owner, Porter Gilbert, who moved to Logan County around 1795. Sold in 1802 to a Butler Rush of Logan County, in 1819 or 1820 "he was licensed to preach as a Methodist minister."[8]

In her mid-fifties herself by this time, Clara would similarly have received the honorific bestowed on many elderly black women—"Aunt." With the traits of goodness and kindness later recognized in Colorado already long since developed, "Aunt" Clara Brown was surely respected and loved within the Brown household and Russellville.

Once again, however, her faith was put to the test. In 1856, George Brown died. His will exists today, in Will Book H, p. 35, in the Logan County courthouse in Russellville. It contains the first printed mention of Clara: she is one of three slaves identified, and was to receive $300. The wife, Martha, was to receive a "Dowry" of $3,463.35, with an additional $1,732.63 to be divided among the wife and three children. The remainder of the estate consisted of the brick house off the public square and various land holdings.

For Clara, this was an event at once traumatic and liberating. The Brown home had been hers for 20 years. As the bequest of $300 (a considerable sum in those days) indicates, she was well thought of by the family. Indeed, with the growing separation from her own children—she had probably lost track of them all by this time—they were in a real sense the only family she had.

But again, economic factors intruded. Clara was, at her age, more of a liability than an asset from a slaveholder's perspective. Her price on the auction block was likely to be minimal. On the other hand, the Brown daughters now had families of their own (assuming that Lucinda and her son would have returned to her late husband's parents upon the death of George Brown). None of them was likely in a position to welcome an elderly slave into the household.

It would be nice to think that Christian charity, rather than a dollars-and-cents analysis, was the primary factor in their thinking, but in any case the daughters worked with Clara to arrange her manumission. The account in the *Republican* is convoluted, but does seem to have some basis in fact. The entire narration is as follows:

> The children did not know how soon the family might be broken up, and they wanted to see Clara placed in a position where she could not be sold to other parties as a slave. It was, therefore, determined to sell Clara from the block. The three daughters agreed to donate their interest, leaving the slave only to pay one-fourth of the sum for which she sold. The immediate members of the household had an understanding that the bid for her was not to exceed $12—leaving the slave only $3 to pay in order to gain her freedom. This arrangement to sell Clara from the block was made in order to comply with the law of the day and legalize her freedom. The day of the sale rolled around, and Colonel Hockersmith, the well-known Kentucky crier, conducted the sale. The plan adopted by the Browns did not carry out according to the original programme, other bidders putting in an appearance, and the Browns were compelled to bid $475 in order to prevent her going out of the family. The three Misses Brown, however, released their interests in favor of the colored woman, leaving Clara to pay the other fourth—$119. The woman had saved up nearly $100 and she paid this over and was legally released from slavery. The three young ladies married a short time after this, and dispersed to different sections.[9]

This account seems to swell with authentic detail, which we would assume the writer took from Aunt Clara's own words. However, in those few details that can be checked against existing records, the *Republican* account is so clearly in error that we are inclined to look suspiciously upon the rest.

To start at the end, while the narrative indicates that "[t]he three young ladies married a short time after this, and dispersed to different sections," Logan County marriage records demonstrate that all three of the daughters had been married for some years by this time, though one had been widowed.

In the previous sentence, moreover, it is mentioned that Clara had "saved up nearly $100," ignoring the fact that Brown had left Clara $300 in his will. Given these misstatements, the accuracy of the remainder of the account is certainly in question. And the suggestion that some "understanding" existed that she would be sold at a public auction for just $12 makes no sense at all.

We get little help from the other contemporaneous sources, however. Burrell wrote briefly that, after Brown's death, Clara "was again sold and purchased by the heirs of Mr. Brown, and emancipated."[10] Other accounts from the period are equally confusing, one stating that Clara herself "[b]ought her freedom,"[11] while a later *Denver Republican* article said Clara had "been given her freedom."[12]

Another source confuses the issue still further. General Frank Hall was a Colorado pioneer, and one who likely would have known Clara there. He published, together with Ovando Hollister, the Black Hawk *Mining Journal* in the 1860's. Later, he was secretary for a number of the Colorado territorial governors, and still later mining editor for the *Denver Post*. Drawing on this diverse background, he wrote a multi-volume *History of Colorado* in the late 1890's. His loving sketch of Aunt Clara largely follows Burrell, but after mentioning her sale to Brown and the separation from her family in 1835, he adds that upon "the death of this new master she became the property of still another purchaser by whom she was manumitted...."[13]

The consensus would seem to indicate two significant, but somewhat contradictory, points. First, the Brown daughters actively participated in the effort to secure Aunt Clara's freedom. Second, Clara herself either bought her own freedom or financially contributed from her own savings to the process.

At any rate, Clara was now a free woman. The experience must have been at once exhilarating and disorienting. We have no information regarding her activities as a free woman in Kentucky. Assuming she still had some of the money left to her by Brown, it is likely that she spent some of her time, and of those funds, trying to locate her missing children.

Burrell wrote that "[t]he laws of Kentucky then requiring that all emancipated slaves should leave the state within one year,"[14] Clara left the state. But no such laws were cited by Coleman in his *Slavery Times in Kentucky*, written in 1940. What Coleman does document is an oppressive system of law and custom designed to keep the free blacks under the white man's control, and to limit opportunities for runaway slaves to join them. Coleman wrote:

> *Free Negroes were required to have with them at all times and in all places their certificates of freedom, or free papers, and present them for inspection when called upon by the town watch or "patterollers." Usually written on parchment, the certificate set out the name, age and description of the Negro, together with the date and place of his emancipation.*[15]

In leaving Kentucky, Clara may have thought she would be leaving behind such repressive practices. But the 1882 *Republican* interview may have been closer to the truth, saying that "[h]aving no ties to bind her longer, she made arrangements to come West, and she left Kentucky in the latter part of 1856."[16]

It is hard to imagine Aunt Clara leaving behind either of her daughters in Kentucky, if she knew them to be living there. It seems likely, then, that Margaret, who had been living in Morgantown, had passed away by this time, and that Clara believed that Eliza Jane, who had left the service of the Covington family in 1852, had departed the area.

Whether Clara had specific information that suggested that Eliza Jane had already come west, or just thought Missouri to be a likely destination given what she knew of events of the day, the contemporaneous accounts are consistent in saying that she traveled first to St. Louis.[17] Bruyn, as usual, fancifully mixed research of likely routes and means of transportation with a wholly invented scenario of the persons and methods involved.[18] It is true, however, considering the restrictions of public transportation for free blacks, Clara would probably have needed assistance in reaching St. Louis. Perhaps the Brown daughters helped her. And river transportation was the most likely means.

St. Louis was founded as a trading post in 1763. It was part of the vast French overseas empire acquired by the United States with the Louisiana Purchase of 1803. And Missouri itself became a state only in 1820. Despite this relative youth, however, the city Clara arrived at in 1856 was in many ways far more cosmopolitan than anything in Kentucky. St. Louis had long been an important hub for Mississippi River traffic, especially since the first steamboat (named, interestingly enough, after Colorado explorer Zebulon M. Pike) docked there in 1817. With substantial iron deposits nearby, St. Louis became a manufacturing center, and those manufactured goods were shipped downstream through New Orleans and to east coast ports, as well as upstream on flatboats in exchange for furs. Before the Civil War, St. Louis was the third busiest port in the nation.

More important for Clara's situation, the city had become a major staging area for travelers heading further west. Many of the wagon trains heading out over the Oregon Trail, and of the prospectors and miners who streamed westward to California after the discovery of gold at Sutter's Mill in 1849, were outfitted at St. Louis. The area was blessed with substantial German and Irish immigration during this period. And many free blacks, fleeing the increasing persecution and harassment in their home states, joined in this migration.

Most of the earliest settlers of Missouri had come up to the state from the South, and the state's admission to the Union in 1820 as a slaveholding state (paired with Maine, a free state) was a key factor in what became known as the Missouri Compromise. As part of that compromise, no restrictions on free blacks were allowed in the Missouri constitution. Though the provisions dividing the nation's newly acquired territories into slave and free states along the 36° 30' line had been specifically repealed by the Kansas-Nebraska act of 1854, the Missouri constitution was still favorable to free black citizens.

But if Clara and the other free blacks who poured into the state thought that Missouri was a beacon of equality, they were sadly mistaken. Over the years a number of punitive laws had been enacted by various governmental entities that affected Clara and her fellow African-Americans. One law that may have hastened Clara's departure from St. Louis—and at least was indicative of the temper of the town—was Ordinance #4423, ordained by the Common Council of the City of St. Louis on April 1, 1859. Besides several measures pertaining to the relations between slaves and owners, a number of the provisions were particularly pernicious for free blacks.

The law required, for example, that "[a]ny negro or mulatto, bond or free, who shall be found without a pass between the hours of ten o'clock P.M. and four o'clock A.M....abroad in the city from his usual place of abode, unless he be going to or coming from some lawful place of business or lawful assemblage, shall forfeit and pay for the first offense not less than one nor more than five dollars; for the second offense, not less than five nor more than ten dollars; and for every subsequent offense, not less than ten nor more than twenty dollars."

The passes were to be issued by the mayor, for any free black "of good moral character, whose business requires him to be out between the hours above mentioned...." The pass could be revoked at the mayor's pleasure. Nor could blacks "hold, at night, any assemblage without the written permission of the mayor; nor shall they remain at any ball, religious meeting, or other assemblage" after two in the morning.

Whether the passage of this law played any factor in her decision is unknown, but around this time Aunt Clara moved to Leavenworth, Kansas Territory. The *Republican* biography puts the move in 1859,[19] though Burrell wrote that she moved in 1858, spending the year in the Kansas town.[20]

Clara's choice to relocate to Leavenworth makes little sense unless it is viewed in the context of her desire to find information on her missing child, Eliza Jane, and her ultimate decision to move further west, to Colorado. Compared to sophisticated St. Louis, Leavenworth was little more than a frontier outpost.

Colonel Henry Leavenworth founded Fort Leavenworth on the bluffs overlooking the Missouri River in 1827, manning it with the 3rd Infantry Regiment from St. Louis. The primary purpose in locating a fort there was to protect the travelers on the Santa Fe Trail from Indian attacks.

When Kansas Territory was organized in 1854, newly appointed Governor Andrew Reeder set up executive offices at the fort for a time. The town company, the first in the Territory, was organized on June 13, 1854, and in the summer of 1855 the city of Leavenworth was incorporated by special act of the Territorial Legislature. By that time, the population had grown to 500.

But in the next few years, Leavenworth grew at a phenomenal rate. By the fall of 1857 the population had soared to 5,000, and that doubled to 10,000 by the time Clara arrived a year or so later. By the end of 1858, the city was connected by telegraph to Jefferson City and Kansas City, Missouri. But for Clara—as for most of the other new immigrants—the attraction was less what the city itself had to offer than its reputation as the point of embarkation for the various routes to the West. John Gregory, the Georgia prospector who eventually discovered the lode gold that justified the stampede to the Rockies, led a wagon train from Leavenworth to Ft. Laramie that summer.

With the first stirrings of gold rush fever in the Pikes Peak region, William Hepburn Russell organized the Leavenworth & Pikes Peak Express service. It was just one of a number of freighting services started by the "tightly wound promoter who operated on the Missouri frontier."[21] By April of 1859, Concord stagecoaches, built by the Abbot Downing company of Concord, New Hampshire, were regularly traveling the 687-mile route from Leavenworth to the newly established city of Denver, the burgeoning supply center for mining expeditions into the Rockies. The first pair arrived May 7, 1859, and certainly helped fuel the "rush to the Rockies."

(Though initially popular, the service was also extravagantly costly. By 1859 Russell was a half-million dollars in debt. Teaming with old partners Alexander Majors and William B. Waddell, Russell formed the famous Central Overland California and Pikes Peak Express Company in October 1859. The famed Pony Express mail service was a later—and financially disastrous—offering of the same company).

We know little of Clara's life in either St. Louis or Leavenworth. Work would have been plentiful in either location, and it seems likely that by the time of her stay in Leavenworth, at least, Clara had acquired the laundry tubs that were the hallmark of her occupation for the remainder of her life. She had probably long since made back whatever money she had to put toward her manumission from slavery back in Kentucky, and had acquired a tidy bankroll from her labors.

But the move to Leavenworth confirms that Clara intended to move west, rather than being merely swept along by the gold rush. Given her age (by this time she would have been in her late fifties) and the prospects in Missouri and Kansas for steady employment, it seems unlikely that she was caught up in the madness that possessed so many of the pioneer "Argonauts" heading for the Rockies. She must have had some inkling—whether intuition, common sense, or even some information—that led her to believe that her long-lost daughter, Eliza Jane, had also come west. And she was willing to go to great lengths to find her.

Chapter 3

When Clara elected to travel by wagon train to the Pikes Peak country (as the area around Denver was known for the only recognizable landmark in a hundred miles), she was joining a great stream of humanity that was being pushed out of the established United States, and drawn to a vast and largely unknown territory.

Drawing the Argonauts were rumors and reports of gold in the Rockies that had been swirling for years. George F. Willison, detailing the Colorado rush years later, noted that "reports of gold in the mountains begin to multiply.... One circulates in '35, another in '43, a third in '49. Stories begin to be less circumstantial. In '50 Indian traders definitely place gold in Clear Creek and two years later in Ralston Creek nearby."[1]

Many of the initial gold seekers in Colorado had Georgia roots. While largely overshadowed today by the memories of Sutter's Mill and Pikes Peak, of Virginia City and the Klondike, it was a find on Cherokee lands in Georgia in the 1830's that was the new nation's first "gold rush." While a minor discovery compared to these later bonanzas, the take was sufficient to justify establishment of a branch mint at Dahlonega in 1838.

Miners with experience in the Georgia fields would prove instrumental in exploring the Colorado mountains, just as they did in California in 1849. While the story of James Marshall finding the first nugget of gold at Sutter's Mill is well known, it was Isaac Humphreys, a Georgia miner, who proved the area a paying proposition.

Some of the early finds that fanned the flames in Colorado, furthermore, were made by Cherokees who were knowledgeable of—and probably displaced by—the Georgia mining. Pioneer Colorado newspaperman Ovando Hollister, promoting the mines of Colorado in an 1867 book of that name, reported:

> *A party of Cherokee Indians, traveling overland to Colorado in 1852, via the Arkansas River and along the eastern base of the Sierra Madre to the North Platte at Fort Laramie, by some means found gold in the banks of Ralston Creek, a small affluent of the Vasquez Fork of the South Platte, emptying into it near its mouth; and each year thereafter parties of Cherokees had gone out and prospected the streams in the vicinity of what is now Denver City. At last they were successful; they obtained a few dollars' worth of the glittering dust, which they carried home late in 1857, exhibiting it freely as they passed through Nebraska into Kansas.*[2]

These may have been the same parties of which Willison wrote, "[f]inally in '54 or '55 a band of Western Cherokees, accompanied by two Ralston brothers from Georgia, come north from Indian territory in search primarily of good buffalo country in which to settle. But as all know something of mining, they have an eye out for gold as well...."[3]

Other Indians, too, had a part in starting the contagion. Fall Leaf, a Delaware Indian, passed through Lawrence, Kansas, in 1857 with a quantity of gold he claimed to have found in the Rockies.

With these tantalizing displays, organized parties set out for the Rockies almost simultaneously from the mining fields of Georgia and the border settlements of Kansas Territory. One such party, from Georgia, was headed by William Green Russell, an experienced Georgia miner who had also spent time in the California fields. On an earlier trip to California, the Green Russell party left the established Santa Fe Trail, headed north along the Arkansas River, and pushed north along the mountains to Fort Laramie, where they rejoined the Overland Trail. "Panning for gold in every stream they crossed, they first 'raised color' on the South Platte at the mouth of a small sandy creek lined with choke cherries—the renowned Cherry Creek of later years. Again their pans showed color at the mouth of Cache La Poudre forty miles to the north. But in neither instance were the colors sufficient to divert them from their goal."[4]

But this trip was different, with the Rockies the goal, not merely a diversion. Green Russell and his men arrived around the 1st of June 1858, at the mouth of Cherry Creek. Prospecting north and south from that base, they found encouraging signs of gold in many streams, but were unable to ascertain its source.

While the Green Russell party was away in the mountains, wagon trains of Kansas settlers began arriving at Cherry Creek. Not themselves skilled in prospecting, they quickly attached themselves to the Green Russell group. One of their number, John King, rode back to Lawrence, home to many in the first Kansas expedition, and spoke vaguely but tantalizingly of the prospects.

As Willison put it, "King's secret is not long kept. All Lawrence quickly knows it and neighboring towns as well. It early reaches the ears of the Larimers, private bankers and dealers in land warrants at Leavenworth. Here at Leavenworth the greatest excitement prevails. Street corners are crowded far into the night with men eagerly discussing routes and equipment necessary for a dash to the 'Kansas Gold Fields.' Leavenworth, it seems, is about to be depopulated."[5]

Willison's description was echoed in the local Leavenworth newspaper, the *Kansas Weekly Herald*. "On the headwaters of the South Fork of Platte, near Long's Peak, gold mines have been discovered and 500 persons are now working them. These mines are now yielding on an average $12 a day to each hand. They are 175 miles from Fort Laramie, and 25 from St. Vrain's Fort, in Nebraska."[6]

As noted earlier, we can't know exactly when Aunt Clara arrived in Leavenworth. But this is the excited atmosphere into which she came. General

William Larimer was among the first arrivals in Cherry Creek, and on November 22, 1858, platted a town site named Denver (after the short-term Kansas governor James W. Denver) to compete with the Georgians' Auraria. Larimer was nothing if not a world-class promoter (self-promoter, more accurately) and he made sure that glowing reports of the town's prospects got back to the Kansas settlements. While it was still just a patch of barren dirt, Larimer wrote home to the mayor of Leavenworth that Denver was "bound to be a great city."

But as Larimer's presence would indicate, not all were drawn by the lure of gold. Even those who remained in Kansas "were only too eager to stimulate a boom that would bring business to the little towns that would become the points of departure for Colorado."[7]

Many were anxious just to escape the dreadful economic conditions following the Panic of 1857. As historian James Grafton Rogers wrote, "[t]he strain of frontiersmen who had halted their rapid movement west—their homes had been moved a thousand miles in a century—were fretting in the half-settled and conventional farm lands which were so at variance with their inheritance of seeking rainbows beyond the sunset. The panic of 1857 upset even the steadiest of them. There was no market for their farm crops and stores denied them credit for shoes and tools. Young men, even educated men, lawyers and doctors, could establish no footing. Suddenly rumors of wealth in the Rocky Mountains, then proof of it, then all the promise of freedom, enterprise and opportunity that a new frontier presents, broke the dam."[8]

Samuel Cushman, writing in 1876, put the situation even more poetically: "The year 1857 was, financially, a bad one. Thousands were in a wilderness of debt, waiting for a Moses, and dreaming of a promised land."[9]

The lust for gold was a factor in igniting the gold rush fever, but it was by no means the entire reason. "It seems obvious that the yellow flakes found in Cherry Creek are not the whole or even the real story. The early discoveries only released forces that were accumulated already in the states east of the Missouri and Mississippi Rivers. The first gold found was trivial in quantity and not at all the same as the mountain deposits which later produced wealth."[10] And mining historian Rodman Paul observed that "there was no substantial basis for the initial excitement."[11]

But such niceties mattered little to the unemployed professionals and landless farmers wiped out by the Panic of 1857. Even the mere suggestion of wealth was better than what they were leaving behind. The combination of gold's allure and financial desperation produced something very like a mob mentality. The Reverend W. H. Goode, pastor of a church in Lawrence, Kansas, when the craze was at its height, described it thus: "Some were thoughtful, prudent men—men who, under other circumstances, might have succeeded; but the great mass were inconsiderate, rash, and reckless, with indifferent teams, poor, crazy wagons, and almost without harnesses. A large number of men actually harnessed themselves to hand-carts, as beasts of burden, to draw their tools, provisions, and equipage, almost a thousand miles over a uninhabited plain; some undertook the journey with wheelbarrows, while not a few hazarded the entire trip, from some of the more remote States, on foot, lugging their tent-poles and scanty supplies upon their shoulders."[12]

Even experienced historians, writing some seventy years later, were amazed by the frenzy. One wrote, "[n]o other period in our history can furnish a spectacle similar to the handcart exodus from Leavenworth to Denver, while the craze was at its height. Men, women and children, with their belongings tumbled into a handcart (because they lacked horses), started on the dangerous six hundred mile trip across the Plains toward an uncertain future."[13]

The flames were further fanned by the appearance in Kansas and elsewhere of a number of guidebooks on how to get to the Pikes Peak country, and the riches that awaited there. "Apparently two guidebooks to the Pike's Peak gold region were published in the fall of 1858.... Seventeen guidebooks to the Pike's Peak region were issued in 1859. The wide distribution of these books and the general interest in the subject treated, are in part indicated by the places of publication. Five were issued from New York City, three from Chicago, two from Cincinnati, and one each from Boston, Pittsburgh, Pacific City (Iowa), Washington, Leavenworth, and St. Louis."[14]

Whether Clara was aware of the Leavenworth guidebook or any of the others matters little, for she was surely aware of the wonders the books described. By these accounts, Denver was soon to be the next great metropolis of the western hemisphere and it was probably this promised growth, rather than the rumored riches in the mountain mining camps, that interested Clara. Here, she may have thought, was a prospect that might attract her Eliza Jane. Leaving her frontier Kansas home behind, Clara set off for the Pikes Peak region in the spring of 1859.

The accounts of her passage in both Burrell and the *Denver Republican* are similar, though Burrell gave many more details:

> *Early in 1859, she joined the gold hunting army for Auraria, Cherry Creek, now Denver, she agreeing to cook for a mess of twenty-five men out of a party of sixty, the conditions being that they transport her stoves, wash-tubs, wash-board and clothes-box, for her services as cook during the trip. She rode with her things in one of the ox-wagons, there being thirty in the train, drawn by six yoke of oxen each, and, after eight weeks, landed in Auraria, now West Denver.*[15]

And an army it indeed was, setting out from the Missouri River towns for the distant Pikes Peak region. Reverend Goode estimated that "during the months of April and May, one hundred thousand persons crossed the Missouri River. Some went nearly through, others half-way, but by far the larger number only a short distance into the Territory, encountering severe rains, snow-storms, and other hardships and exposures."[16] Writing from a more recent perspective, a twentieth-century historian came up with a similar number: "It is estimated that of the 100,000 goldseekers who set out from the Missouri River in the spring of 1859, about 50,000 reached the mountains, and about half of these returned home shortly after reaching Cherry Creek."[17]

Even in the best-prepared and organized trains, the trip was a difficult one. Depending on route, weather conditions and obstacles encountered along the way, passage took somewhere around eight weeks, as did Clara's train. A number of travelers kept diaries, which have since been published, or sent letters back to their hometown newspapers, chronicling the hardships encountered along the way. Clara is said to have arrived in Denver on June 6, 1859, which would indicate a departure date somewhere around the middle of April. She may well have been on the trail on May 6, 1859. On that date, another Georgian, John Gregory, made the discovery of lode gold that finally proved true the rumors of fabulous wealth that had stirred the settlers to migration in the first place.

We have no particular details on the journey Aunt Clara made; the name of a "Colonel Wadsworth" has come down to us as the wagonmaster, but Bruyn's correspondence with the Kansas State Historical Society failed to reveal any records of him.[18] We will never know if her voyage was particularly grueling, or blessed with fair weather and good conditions. But in any case, given the number of failures cited by Goode and others, the fact that Clara arrived successfully is a testament to her ability to choose a reputable wagonmaster—as well as to her own drive and stamina. Still, for a woman now nearing sixty years old, the journey must have been a trial.

By this time, as noted earlier, Russell and his partners were already running regular, comfortable stagecoach service to Denver. The trip that took Clara a month or two could have been made in a matter of days. Then why didn't Clara, who almost certainly had sufficient funds for her passage, go by stage?

We must remember, unfortunately, that though this new Trans-Mississippi West was in many ways a place of great freedom and tolerance, it was at the same time part of the ante-bellum United States. Clara, like all African-Americans, would not have been welcome as a paying passenger in a public conveyance. Her service as cook to the company she joined was less a matter of economic than of social necessity.

Finally, we come to one last unanswered question regarding Clara's emigration from Kansas, and it comes to us from a previously unmentioned "biographer."

James Thomson was an Englishman by birth, a poet by profession and a mine manager by necessity. Still comparatively unknown in England by the early 1870's, despite having contributed "many pieces and scraps in prose and verse"[19] to the *National Reformer*, Thomson made ends meet by working in a variety of positions in London. He "had been employed as clerk in various offices, as proofreader in a printing office, and finally as secretary of the British mining company officially known as the Champion Gold and Silver Mining Company of Colorado."[20]

British ownership of Colorado mining interests had become common by the early 1870's; one author listed 14 such companies in 1871.[21] Londoner William Green purchased the Champion and California gold mines in Gilpin County, outside Central City, in August 1871, for £38,000, forming the joint stock company mentioned above in December. Thomson was hired as the new company's secretary, and arrived in May of 1872 as "the Company's representative."[22]

Thomson was a keen observer of human society, and an obsessive diarist; he kept both a business and a personal diary during his stay in Central City, and a photocopy of the latter is kept at the University of Colorado. The first entry in his personal journal was a recollection of his conversation, during a coach ride back from Central City, with an "old coloured woman...Aunty (Clara or Cary?) she is called, well known and respected in Central."[23]

Thomson's account of his months in Central City is always lively, but sometimes fanciful, or at least exaggerated. We can assume that he didn't try writing while bouncing around the "jerky" they were traveling in, but jotted down his recollection of the day's events that evening, or the following morning. Bruyn was familiar with his description of Aunt Clara, and dismissed it with a handwritten note: "Bunk!"

And certainly there are errors in his account, which could be attributed to his writing from memory several hours after the conversation. He wrote, for example, that Clara "lost her husband and children (two others died young)," which contradicts all the other accounts of her family that mention only the premature death of Paulina, Eliza Jane's twin. But it is correct in the essentials of her life to that date, and is in many respects the most revealing and personal of the descriptions we have of Aunt Clara written during her lifetime.

So it's worth examining Thomson's recounting of Aunt Clara's emigration to Colorado, where he wrote, "[b]ought her freedom in '56, came out here with two other negresses, in '59...." No other contemporaneous account says anything about any other black women traveling with her. So it was easy enough for Bruyn to dismiss this revelation.

But why would Thomson have come up with such a notion at all, unless Clara had mentioned it to him? The diaries were never intended for publication, and none of the other accounts of her life had yet been printed. Moreover, re-reading the other contemporaneous accounts gives no particular reason to doubt Thomson's version, though Burrell did refer to Clara as "the first colored woman that ever crossed the plains."[24] Conversely, we have no other accounts to support Thomson's unique assertion.

But, interestingly, there seem to have been very early in the Pikes Peak settlements two other African-American women, both identified as laundresses. Is it possible that these women accompanied Clara in her trip across the plains?

One of the women is a rather shadowy figure, a minor character in the saga of the great black mountain man, Jim Beckwourth. Beckwourth is a legendary presence in the early history of the Rocky Mountain West, a contemporary of Kit Carson and Jim Bridger. He wrote his own memoirs, and several books have been written about him since.

Beckwourth was somewhat of a free spirit, and before the extensive immigration spurred by the 1858-1859 gold rush, he had a series of Crow women he lived with as husband and wife. But with the growth of the Pikes Peak settle-

22

ments, the aging mountain man decided to settle down and move to the growing towns. There he "became acquainted with Miss Elizabeth Ledbetter, daughter of the first laundress in Denver, and they were married by A. O. McGrew, Esq., on June 21, 1860."[25]

Various accounts of this marriage described the new Mrs. Beckwourth as white, black, or Hispanic.[26] Now while the frontier settlements may have been tolerant, they were not likely to overlook the marriage of a black man, however famous, with a white woman.[27] General Larimer, in his later *Reminiscences*, recalled that Beckwourth "went to a place on Clear Creek near the present site of Denver. It was here that he married a colored woman and built him a house...."[28] Willison also mentioned that Beckwourth killed a man when he "objected to his attentions to the comely young negress known as 'Lady' Beckwourth."[29] And Ledbetter (Lettbetter in the *Rocky Mountain News* announcement) is hardly a Spanish surname. So it seems likely that Miss Ledbetter was a black woman.

This raises the question of her mother, identified as "the first laundress in Denver." If Aunt Clara worked as a laundress during her brief period in Denver, then apparently this woman was present there at least as early. Could this have been one of the women who crossed the plains with Aunt Clara? Assuming that Elizabeth was of the usual marrying age, the mother would have been probably around 40 years old at the time, or nearly 20 years younger than Clara. Could this woman, and her daughter, have been the "two negresses" Thomson wrote of?

Another possible candidate for one of Aunt Clara's companions is only slightly less obscure. The death of Jennie Spriggs (Golden) was noted briefly in the Central City newspaper, where it was written that "[s]he had been in this county since 1860...."[30] A much later account described that when Jennie "was nineteen, her master gave him to his oldest son. The young man, sowing his wild oats, ran afoul of the law. He and Jennie left Missouri one jump ahead of a posse. It was 1860 and tales of gold lured him to Denver."[31]

This later article continues that, with Jennie in tow, the young man "joined the other gold seekers along Clear Creek in Jefferson and Gilpin counties."[32] There is much in this undocumented narrative, written fifty years after Jennie's death, to make us skeptical; by 1860, for example, the lode gold had been discovered by John Gregory and there was very little prospecting along Clear Creek. More obviously, the notion of a hunted man on the run bringing a household slave—a woman, at that—seems unlikely. Is it possible that this account is largely concocted, and that Jennie arrived in Gilpin County by less dramatic means? And even if the Gilpin County arrival date of 1860 is correct, could not she have come to Denver a year earlier—and with Clara?

Certainly these questions can't now be answered. But the possibility that Thomson's assertion, previously ignored in all the writings about Aunt Clara Brown, has foundation in fact cannot, and should not, be ignored any longer. The picture of not one, but three or four black women—one elderly, one middle-aged, and one or two in her late teens—riding bravely on a wagon train to the unknown Rocky Mountains is an appealing one. That they would have banded together to support each other in the great adventure of crossing the plains should hardly be surprising. Such a conjecture does nothing to diminish our respect for the courage and spirit that Clara showed in making such a journey; it only reflects the sense of Christian charity, and of racial solidarity, that she demonstrated throughout the rest of her life.

Chapter 4

We don't know for sure when Clara arrived in the Cherry Creek settlements that were the destination of the wagon trains from back in "the states." Nor do we know exactly how long she stayed there before moving to the mining camps in the mountains. But we know that this was a productive time for her, and that the contacts she made in her work with the fledgling religious organizations of the towns served her well for the remainder of her life in Colorado.

Certainly some of her biographers made her stay in Denver seem little more than a stopover; Burrell wrote, for instance, that "[a]fter a few weeks' rest, she again packed up her earthly goods and removed to Gregory Point,"[1] as the area near where John Gregory made his momentous discovery of lode gold was sometimes known. The account in the *Republican* skips her time in Denver altogether, saying only that she "located in Central City."[2]

At this time, the confusion was understandable. Denver and Auraria were little more than staging areas for expeditions into the mountains. At the beginning of the year 1859, Denver had perhaps 75 buildings. And even these were subject to sudden disappearances, as unoccupied cabins were often "jumped" by squatters, who erected their own structures.

Even whole towns disappeared. The St. Charles town company was established in September, 1858. When Larimer and his Kansans arrived in November, they simply platted their town on the same land, offering shares in their company for the displaced St. Charles stockholders. Similarly, they offered nine shares, and 53 lots, to Russell's Leavenworth & Pikes Peak Express Company, in exchange for making Denver, rather than Auraria, the terminus of the stagecoach line.[3]

With such shenanigans by the city fathers, it's no surprise that the Cherry Creek communities were renowned for their lawlessness. Gambling and prostitution flourished, and violence was a frequent solution to disputes. By the spring of 1859, as the trickle of Argonauts turned into a full-fledged flood, the settlements degenerated into near chaos. The *Kansas City Journal of Commerce* correspondent wrote of Auraria in 1859 that "[t]here is more drinking and gambling here [in one day] than in Kansas City in six—in fact about one-half the population do nothing else but drink whiskey and play cards."[4]

By June, things grew even more chaotic; an Illinois correspondent wrote home that "[t]housands of cattle, hundreds of wagons and tents, and people innumerable throng the valley of the stream. We find representatives from nearly every state in the Union; there are gaming tents, restaurants, stores, little doggeries where poor whisky is retailed at '10 cents a nip,' itinerant gunsmiths, extempore blacksmith shops; and a general paraphernalia of business is going on."[5]

As the goldseekers began to pour out of the Missouri River settlements and cross the plains to the Pikes Peak country, the Methodist clergy convened in the Fourth Annual Kansas-Nebraska Methodist Conference in Omaha took notice. They dispatched two pastors to the gold fields—Reverend Goode, from Lawrence, and Reverend Jacob Adriance, from Missouri. Though just 23 years old at the time, Adriance enjoyed the courage of his convictions, and he and Goode made the plains crossing in just four weeks, arriving in Denver on June 28, 1859.

Adriance and Goode immediately set to preaching to the restless multitudes, holding their first service in Denver on July 3. While Adriance and Goode traveled frequently to the booming mining camps, Adriance wrote in his diary that they also "kept up prayer meetings on Thursday evenings at my cabin, or at 'Aunt' Clara Brown's cabin, a pious colored lady."[6] In the fall of that year, there were a series of religious meetings held. "Aunt Clara Brown, a colored woman, was the only woman who took part in these meetings."[7]

As the Cherry Creek settlements continued to thrive, more and more families began to arrive, many with children of various ages. With the assistance of the Reverend George W. Fisher, another Methodist minister from Missouri, a "Union" Sunday School was begun. William Byers' *Rocky Mountain News* promoted the upcoming meeting, describing it as the "[f]irst session of a Sunday School ever held in Denver."[8] The class was held November 6, 1859; twelve children attended, and six adults, including "the old colored lady Aunt Clara Brown."

So we can conclude that Aunt Clara was in Denver for at least six months; considering the extreme weather and primitive living conditions in the mining camps where she headed next, it's likely that she remained in Denver through the winter, migrating the following spring. At any rate, she was in the area long enough to establish herself as a laundress. Reverend Adriance, remembering her in a much later letter, seemed to have been writing about her time in Denver when he observed that the "sporting fraternity largely fraternized her washing."[9]

Bruyn, suggesting a connection between Aunt Clara and the early Methodist Church member Henry Reitze, had her working at Reitze's City Bakery in Auraria, one of the early businesses in the settlements that advertised in William Byers' newborn *Rocky Mountain News*.[10] But she also claimed Clara left for the mountains before the end of 1859, which seems unlikely. However long it may have been, throughout her time in Denver she would have been associating with some of the clergy and laymen of the towns, many of whom would become prominent in the state of Colorado in later years.

At the first Sunday School session, for example, the adults who attended—besides Clara and the two pastors—are identified in Isaac Beardsley's history of Colorado Methodism as "Lewis N. Tappin, D. W. Collier, [and] O. F. Goldrich."[11]

Working, no doubt, from Adriance's handwritten diary, Beardsley managed to mangle all three of the names. Lewis Northey Tappan (not Tappin) was from the fourth generation of an illustrious Massachusetts family. A freestater who had arrived in Lawrence with others from Massachusetts involved in the struggle that led to the Kansas-Nebraska Act, after two years there he emigrated to Denver in October of 1859. Independently wealthy, he was a leading pioneer merchant, capitalist and philanthropist, and wrote for both local and eastern newspapers. Like Clara, he too later went to Central City, where he was credited with building the first ore reduction works in the territory.[12]

Pioneer newspaperman O. J. Goldrick (not O. F. Goldrich) was one of the most colorful characters in a frontier Denver that was full of them. He reportedly arrived in an ox cart, which he drove by cracking a bullwhip and cursing in Latin, while wearing "neatly pressed Prince Albert coat over spotless white linen, which in turn tucked into fashionably tight, striped trousers. White high button gaiters topped his glossy shoes. And he wore a black silk stovepipe hat which he cocked over one eye with a kid-gloved hand."[13]

An Irishman educated at Dublin University, Goldrick became Denver's first schoolteacher before settling into a more suitable life as a journalist. His association with the Sunday School must have been out of his natural affinity for children, as he otherwise seemed to lack religious conviction.

But the figure from that first Sunday School session who probably had the closest relationship with Aunt Clara was the other man mentioned, David C. (not W.) Collier. Collier was born in Chautauqua County, New York, in October of 1832, so he had just turned 27 at the time of this session. He attended Oberlin College in Ohio, graduating in August 1857. Oberlin was an extremely progressive institution of its day, admitting students "irrespective of color" from its beginnings in 1833, and women as early as 1837; the three women who graduated in 1841 were the first females in America to receive A.B. degrees, while by the turn of the century one-third of all African-American graduates of predominantly white institutions in the United States had graduated from Oberlin.

Collier then moved to Leavenworth, though probably in advance of Clara, before settling in Wyandotte to study law. Receiving his law degree in October 1858, he promptly left from Kansas City for Denver, arriving December 5.[14] He was supposedly the first lawyer to practice in Denver, and remained in the Cherry Creek area until July 1862, when he moved to Central City and resumed his legal practice there.

Like everyone else in gold rush Colorado, though, Collier was always busy investigating prospective mines in the mountains: Burrell wrote that his "summers were spent in mining, and on exploring expeditions through Gilpin and Clear Creek Cos."[15] Collier also dabbled in real estate, "having built the first house on the east side of Cherry Creek and became the owner of considerable property there at that time."[16] He did likewise in Central City, and his log cabin on High Street, built in 1860, is reputedly the oldest house still standing in that historic mining camp.[17]

Clara may have dealt with Collier in either of these capacities, utilizing his legal services in Denver or Central City, or purchasing some of the Denver lots or mining interests that she came to own from him. But Clara certainly worked with Collier in his later years as editor and publisher of the preeminent Central City newspaper, the *Register*. The paper had been started as a four-page broadsheet, the *Tri-Weekly Miners Register*, in July 1862. Collier began writing editorials for the paper shortly after his arrival, and became associate editor "[o]n his 30th birthday, October 13, 1862."[18]

Over the following years, Collier assumed, in partnership with various other parties, ownership of the paper, which changed over that period. It published both daily and weekly editions, and dropped the "Miners" from the masthead in 1868.[19] Clara's name appeared occasionally in the paper during that period, so we may assume that she and Collier maintained their friendship over the years. Collier was associated with the Congregational Church in Central City when it was organized,[20] and it may well have been through that connection that Clara came to give the building fund a $100 contribution.

But certainly the most controversial association Clara may have made in her Denver stay was with another central figure in the Colorado history of the Methodist Church, John Milton Chivington. Chivington arrived in Denver in May 1860, by which time Clara may have been in Central City. But she would undoubtedly have come to know him in her church activities there, if she missed him in Denver.

With such a given name, it might be presumed that Chivington had a religious upbringing, but the faith seems to have had little impression on him as a young man. He was born on an Ohio farm in 1821; his father died when he was only five, so he received scant education, his services being needed more on the family homestead. One of his later defenders, Jacob Piatt Dunn, Jr., wrote of him in his book *Massacres in the Mountains*:

> At a log-rolling in the neighborhood a good old Methodist brother reproved him one day for profanity, and the sturdy youth answered defiantly: "I will swear when I please and where I please." But he brooded over the rebuke, and a few days later he went to his reprover's house, determined to swear there before his family. He did not do as he intended. Some unknown power beat down his resolution and the curse died trembling on his tongue. He went away, but the mysterious influence followed him. His eyes were turned inward on his guilty soul; he could not rest. He struggled against it, but in vain, and soon he sought at the altar the pardon for his sins.[21]

This religious conversion marked a pronounced change in Chivington's life. He joined the Methodist Church, and was ordained as a minister in 1844. He was ordered first to Illinois, then to Missouri where his combative temperament—and his strident opposition to slavery and secession—made him many enemies. Partly for his own safety, he was sent to Omaha, where he remained until he was dispatched to Denver as Presiding Elder of the Rocky Mountain District of the Methodist Episcopal Church South on March 14, 1860. Though charged primarily as an administrator, Chivington took every opportunity to preach, as well.

But even in this position his pugnacious personality caused suspicion; one author even named him (along with General Larimer, *Rocky Mountain News* publisher William Byers and others) as a possible member of a group of vigilantes that used hangings to enforce order in the rowdy pioneer settlements.[22]

Clara would have no doubt been impressed, as were most Denverites, with the ruddy Scotch-Irishman's physical presence, and welcomed his staunch opposition to slavery. But his willingness to cast off his clerical garb in favor of a military uniform would have likely appalled her, and his noted antipathy to Colorado's Native American residents would have horrified her. At one point (speaking to a gathering of church deacons, no less!), he roared: "It simply is not possible for Indians to obey or even understand any treaty. I am fully satisfied, gentlemen, that to kill them is the only way we will ever have peace and quiet in Colorado."

If Clara heard of such statements, she would have been particularly offended, for she always claimed to be of Indian descent. A much later *Denver Republican* article read that "Aunt Clara stated that her grandparents were Indian,"[23] and commentators frequently remarked on her Indian appearance. The same article stated that Clara "was never in the least afraid of them, and often entertained them at her house."[24]

The future would hold both honor and disgrace for Chivington. At the outbreak of the Civil War, Territorial Governor William Gilpin offered him a chaplaincy, which he declined in order to take a "fighting" commission. As a Major with the 1st Colorado Volunteer Regiment, he earned fame as the hero who planned the surprise attack that won the battle of Glorietta Pass in New Mexico, saving the gold fields of Colorado from a rebel attack. Active politically, he was spoken of as one of Colorado's first congressional representatives, or even governor, when the statehood that was seen as imminent was granted.

His prospects were dashed a few months later, however, when on November 29, 1864, Chivington's troops attacked and massacred a peaceful band of Cheyenne camping at Sand Creek. While never formally punished for his actions (and, in fact, initially lauded by the Denver papers and populace), as details of the massacre began to emerge, Chivington was investigated, condemned, and ultimately vilified. An Army judge declared that the action was "a cowardly and cold-blooded slaughter, sufficient to cover its perpetrators with indelible infamy, and the face of every American with shame and indignation."

But that was all years in the future; we will never know whether Clara saw hints of the violence that apparently lay buried in the heart of the new Methodist minister. Still later, though, Chivington, having remained active in the Colorado Pioneer Association, used his influence within the organization to assist and later, upon her death, honor the ex-slave he would have met in his first few weeks in the Pikes Peak country. It could be that, having faced the devil in his own soul, Chivington recognized the angelic nature of Clara's. Unfortunately, it seems in her life of service and piety she was a model that, however much he may have admired, he chose not to emulate.

Chapter 5

However much Clara might have been amazed by the gold fever that swept through Leavenworth, or shocked by the wide-open and lawless lifestyle of the Cherry Creek settlements, neither would have prepared her for what she found when she arrived at the mining camps. A string of ramshackle "cities" had spread out from the area where John Gregory's initial gold discovery in May, 1859, was now a year old.

Even the voyage to the camps was a thing of wonderment. The Reverend Goode described it on one of his preaching missions about that time:

> *The road presents one continued stream of travel; wagons, carts, footmen, going, returning; horses, mules, oxen, cows, men, packed to the utmost stretch of capacity; breeching to the body of every animal capable of wearing such harness, even sometimes to the riding saddles; the road filled with dust, coal-blackened by the late mountain fires, and visages so begrimed that every downward passenger might well be taken for a collier just emerging from his subterranean cavern. It is computed that five hundred persons pass over this road daily. And this is the "new road," the improved road, the older being almost entirely abandoned because of its still greater difficulty.*[1]

Echoing Goode's sentiments, Hollister also noted how greatly improved the roads were by 1860: "Very fair roads had been made into the Mountains—one *via* Golden Gate, one *via* Bradford. They were not so perfect as now, but were a vast improvement upon the first hill-road, over which in places twenty yoke of oxen were required to *climb*, without dragging anything worth mentioning, perhaps a wagon containing a sack of flour.... On the 4th of March, 1860, Kehler & Montgomery's express coach arrived in the mines from Denver, the first ever run on the line."[2]

As usual, we have no exact record as to when Clara arrived, nor do we know exactly how she traveled. However, it probably was not by one of the comparatively speedy, comfortable stagecoaches. Some years later, the Central City paper noted that as late as 1865 "the coach line between here and Denver refused to carry colored people,"[3] prior to the passage of the federal civil rights law in 1866. Once again, despite having money with which to pay, Clara would have been denied transportation on a "public conveyance."

Given the hordes of vehicles of all sorts that Goode described, however, and the fact that Clara had money more than adequate for such a comparatively short trip, there were a number of ways in which she might have accomplished the journey. Most likely, since she had already acquired the tools of her trade—the "stoves, wash-tubs, wash-board and clothes-box"[4] that Burrell wrote that she brought with her from Kansas—she would have hired a wagon and driver to ferry her property to Mountain City. This would be all the more likely if, as remains possible, she was accompanied by Jennie Spriggs, who by all accounts began her career as a laundress in Black Hawk about the same time.

Similarly, we don't know where Clara first took up residence, or began her business. Burrell wrote that she "removed to Gregory Point, thence to Mountain City, now Central City."[5] The distinctions are, at most, academic; there were no fixed boundaries for any of the settlements in the area, none of the "cities" having been formally surveyed or incorporated. Caroline Bancroft, writing much later, even put her initial arrival in Black Hawk,[6] but that may be because the site of Gregory's initial discovery, commemorated with a monument in 1932, actually lay within the city limits of that community when it was incorporated in 1864.[7]

Clara's earliest recorded property transaction, however, was in the area known as Mountain City. Lying immediately alongside the Gregory lode, this "city" consisted mainly of two streets paralleling the lode, along Packard Gulch, with a third street running east and west along Gregory Gulch. The town site was platted by Richard Sopris, and the first cabin built May 22, 1859, just two weeks after John Gregory's initial discovery. The "City" boomed; a later writer described it this way:

> The infant "City" was a tremendous confusion of log cabins, tents, lean-to's, wickiups, wagon boxes, packing boxes; in fact any article which would afford protection from the weather was utilized for shelter. Mixed in with all this were crude hastily built store buildings of green whip-sawed lumber.[8]

In October, 1860, Clara bought, for $50 in cash, a building lot "described as the 1st lot west of the new one and a half story log house built by Cook and McBride and recorded on the records of said Mountain City as the 3rd lot above the Mountain City Boarding House on California Street (South Side)...."[9] Clara apparently had a house built on the lot shortly thereafter; when she sold the property in 1868 (for $500!), the deed noted the sale included "the house built by me 1860."[10]

The exact location of the property is impossible to determine at this time; even California Street is gone today. With the exception of a few remaining buildings along Gregory Gulch (later Gregory Street[11] running between Black Hawk and Central City), all the structures on the hillside have long since vanished.[12] Nor do we know how long she may have lived or worked there; within a few years, before the 1868 sale of the Mountain City house, she had acquired additional lots and buildings just west of Mountain City, on Lawrence Street in the newly platted Central City. She also had at least one additional Mountain City lot, buying it in September, 1861, from Thomas White for $90.[13]

Regardless, at that time all the settlements were similar: the distinctive character that separated Black Hawk, Central City, and Nevadaville in later years had yet to be formulated. This was truly frontier living at its most elemental level. As one writer put it, "Central City and other 'cities' were little more than a confusion of tents, shacks, and log cabins."[14] And even in the first year, the communities in "Gregory Gulch" had gone through a boom-and-bust cycle as the first loose gold, the "blossom" rock that could be easily retrieved through hydraulic mining, disappeared. Three letters quoted by historian LeRoy Hafen tell the story:

> (July 4, 1859) *"I have been here only one half day, and proceeded up the ravine only about half a mile; it is past all comprehension; I have seen at least 3000 persons, 200 to 300 sluices, and 150 cabins already. I have the most positive information that within six square miles there are from 400 to 600 cabins, and from one to two thousand sluices, mostly in operation, a good saw mill, all done within five weeks, and will be more than double in the next five weeks. There are about 15,000 persons, and at least ten thousand are at work in the mines."*[15]

> (July 30, 1859) *"There are at present about 10,000 men at the mines, of that number perhaps 500 are making money, the greater portion, however, are not making expenses.... Times here at present are dull, the merchants and traders get all the dust, and take it to the States, and persons cannot afford to improve the place yet. We feel sadly the want of capitalists out here, and those who do come and invest will coin money. But there has been so many contradictory reports gone from here, that I suppose they are afraid to risk it."*[16]

> (August 28, 1859) *"The most striking evidence of the retrogression, the Gregory Diggings have experienced of late is, however, furnished by the appearance of the valley itself, in which the former are located. Dozens of idle sluices and slides for transporting 'pay dirt' down the mountain sides to the bank of the brook, abandoned cabins, unworked shafts, waterless ditches, could be seen in every direction. The valley was no longer distinguished for want of elbow-room among its sojourners. Not the twentieth part of the dense mass, which moved up or down its narrow bottom the time of my last visit, remained.... The quartz era—an era, as I firmly believe of unexampled prosperity, is already dawning in the Gregory Mines. Four quartz crushers and grinders, two of which are propelled by water, and the third by 'ox' power; commenced operation a few days previous...."*[17]

The August correspondent was entirely correct; the mines of the

Gregory District were, even as early as late 1859, already entering a new era. Deep rock "quartz" mining required different equipment and far more capital than were available to the earliest prospectors. Shafts many hundreds of feet deep would have to be dug, with hoists and pumps powered by steam engines. The ore, once recovered, would need processing, either in grinding mills that reduced the ore to a powder, or through a variety of smelting methods that needed trained engineers to operate. And all of these required money.

This move away from the footloose, independent prospectors of '59 to the corporate mining that would keep the industry alive for the rest of the century was already making a difference in the towns of the gulch by the time Clara arrived in 1860.

While historians may differ in the particulars, there seems to be general consensus that Central City and its satellites were never "Wild West" towns like Dodge City or Deadwood. Except perhaps for the very earliest days, violence was limited in scope, and the populace peaceable in nature. Even compared to later Colorado boomtowns, early settler and surveyor Hal Sayre thought Central City compared favorably: "I think I should say that Central City never was quite as tough and turbulent a place as were, for example, Leadville and Creede. There were not so many disreputable resorts as in other new mining towns, and while there were occasional shooting scrapes, they were rather far apart, considering the fact that adventurers from all parts of the world were attracted by the gold finds. Even our toughs were pretty good fellows."[18]

Saloons, of course, were still popular gathering places. But with gold so much harder to obtain, the recklessness that was characteristic of the first few months largely disappeared. "'The gambling, which for a while prevailed in the place, has almost ceased,' wrote a miner from Nevadaville. 'The gamblers could not live as we have to—on hope—and so have cleared out to a man.'"[19]

The gulch towns had, to a large extent, become factory towns, populated by working men who had little wish to squander their hard-earned wages and little energy left for dissipation. As one writer summarized it:

> For the small entrepreneur and laborers in the mines, life in Central City was a world not of high culture but of hard days and evenings of backbreaking labor which left little time or energy for more than the simplest of amusements; a world not of gracious living but one of rough clapboard shacks and log cabins, the smell of dirty bodies and dirtier clothes.... [20]

And it was these miners, millworkers and merchants that Clara viewed as her potential customers for her services as a laundress.

Generally, her customers were men. As a woman—much less as a black woman—Clara was in a distinct minority in the mining camps. The stories related of the journey across the plains—once more reliable reporters than the original promoters and guidebook editors began to contribute a more objective view—were enough to discourage most women. Even so hardy a traveler as

Augusta Tabor wrote that "[w]hat I endured on that journey only the women who crossed the plains in '59 can realize."[21]

Nor was it just the journey itself that was lamented. One anonymous female settler, writing home to her father in Illinois, had her letter published in the *Galena Courier*: "If I had known what a journey it was to come out here, I would never have seen the Rocky Mountains. It is too hard for any woman to come here.... My advice to all women is that they had better go to the Poor House than come here.... It is an *awful* hard life here, and I have got enough of Pike's Peak."[22]

But James Grafton Rogers felt that "[t]he scarcity of women in the early years was due more to the fact that the prospectors were unmarried than to any hardships,"[23] and Reverend Goode wrote that "[w]omen bear up under the hardships of frontier life as well or better than men. There are more females here than I should have supposed, especially in the towns."[24]

The numbers of women, and the difficulties they faced, were obviously interpreted by different observers in different ways. But regardless, "if women were a rarity in the camps, they were there virtually from the beginning. They helped shape the institutions of a new town, participated in its social life, and influenced its economic development. Most of these women, at least after the first few weeks, were not soiled doves or hurdy-gurdy girls but wives and mothers. In their opinions and in those of others in the community, their most important function was the establishment of homes and the rearing of children, yet historians have paid virtually no attention to this aspect of the story of the mining frontier."[25]

Besides the increasingly corporate nature of the mining and milling—which helped develop a wage-earning middle class that avoided the excesses of wealth and poverty that distinguished the prospecting days—and the civilizing influence of women and families in the early Gregory Gulch camps, another factor that contributed to the comparatively settled nature of the towns as they developed was the spread of organized religion.

Many of the pioneer preachers who worked in Central City and its environs were the same missionaries Clara had known in Denver—Adriance, Goode, and Chivington, for example. All of these and others had participated in large, open-air religious services and meetings in the very first weeks of the rush to the Gregory "Diggings." Various accounts exist of who preached when and where, and they don't always agree.

Early on, there were no full-time resident ministers, nor any buildings specifically intended for Christian services. Hadley Hall, a two-story building on what was evolving into the Main Street of growing Central City, was a grocery and mining supply store on the ground level. But the upper floor, "was equipped with a stage and rude pine benches, and was the first theatre in the Rocky Mountains. Performances by Mrs. Wakely and her three daughters, billed as the 'Mlle. Haidee Troupe,' were offered to audiences of miners from Gregory's Diggins. The hall served for church services as well, some of the earliest of the Catholic ceremonies being held here."[26] Father Joseph Machebeuf, the legendary prelate who had been dispatched to Colorado from New Mexico by Bishop Lamy, was the priest presiding over these early services.

And just as the buildings did double-duty, so too did many of the pioneer missionaries. As Reverend Goode himself noted, there were "quite a respectable proportion of the clergy of different Churches, who, though engaged in secular pursuits, are generally respected as ministers."[27] Some of the preachers seemed to serve a variety of congregations; early on Goode reported that the Gulch boasted "many church members: Methodists of all types known in the country, Baptists, Presbyterians, Congregationalists, with a number of preachers—miners—of the different persuasions, serving them alternately."[28]

Gradually, more formal organization of congregations appeared, as did full-time resident clergymen. One cleric Clara certainly knew was the Reverend Lewis Hamilton, the Presbyterian pastor who had been instrumental in founding the "Union Sunday School" in Central City as early as 1859. The school was formally chartered in October of 1861, with Reverend Hamilton as superintendent. By January of 1862, Hamilton had organized a Presbyterian Church in Central City. As Burrell documented: "The organization was effected by him through the co-operation of the following named persons, who then enrolled their names as members and adopted the prescribed articles of faith and covenant of the church: William L. Lee, E. W. Wells, F. G. Niles, Mr. Miner, Mary E. Moore, Mrs. Hobbs, and Clara Brown...."[29]

While Clara was a member of this Presbyterian Church, (which was still without a building) it is also known that she was of assistance in the organization of other congregations as well. As noted earlier, she gave $100 to the building fund of the Congregational Church, which numbered among its members David C. Collier, whom she had known from the Union Sunday School in Denver.

Years later, at the dedication of that Congregational church building, Clara again provided financial assistance. Though the congregation had apparently pledged enough money to complete construction, either costs were higher than anticipated, or collections lower. As reported in the *Weekly Miner's Register* of February 19, 1867:

> *Rev. Mr. Crawford presented the condition of the finances to the congregation, starting that the amount still due was $2,424, and requested that it be now made up.... When subscriptions were called the following persons pledged themselves for the following sums:*[30]

Among those listed was Mrs. Clara Brown, with a contribution of another $50. This was the same amount given, for example, by the prosperous and respected superintendent of Black Hawk's vast Bobtail mining and milling complex, Andrew N. Rogers. And it certainly compared favorably to the largest gift of $250, from the famed Teller brothers, Henry and Willard.

Her most recognized contribution today, however, remains to St. James Methodist Church in Central City. The earliest Methodist meetings in the mountains, as noted earlier, were conducted by the traveling missionaries, Reverend

Adriance and Reverend Goode. They were soon joined by the Reverend G. W. Fisher, from Missouri. Burrell wrote that "in 1860...an organization took place, with twenty-seven church members, whose meetings were held in the house of Aunt Clara Brown, the colored pioneer...."[31] Aunt Clara was one of the ten named members of the organization.[32]

Always one of the largest congregations in the area, the Methodists "started building a hewn-log church in the fall and it was opened with appropriate services December 25, 1860."[33] Described as a "puncheon-seated"[34] structure, it burned during the winter of 1861. After that, the congregation took to meeting in Lawrence Hall or, later, the newly constructed county office building and courthouse, Washington Hall. They had morning and evening services on Sunday, and a Wednesday evening prayer meeting; the county charged the congregation $50 per quarter for rent.[35] No doubt Clara attended many of these services.

But while the religious meetings are the recorded activities of Aunt Clara, and no doubt ones that gave her great personal satisfaction, the story of her daily life and work is nowhere told. We are told that her two-room cabin on Lawrence Street, the same one that welcomed the early Methodist meetings, is where she did her washing. As Hall put it, "she opened a laundry. The hearty sympathies of the generous miners being enlisted in her cause, everyone befriended her, so that in a few years by incessant toil and the judicious investment of her earnings, she accumulated a modest fortune."[36] We know from Burrell that she charged "for blue and red flannel shirts 50 cents, and other clothes in proportion."[37]

This was a not insubstantial sum to the workingmen of the region; most miners at the time earned from $2 to $4 a day, depending on specialty and experience. And most prices were, because of the exorbitant shipping costs, high by comparison to costs for similar products back in "the States." When the Reverend William Crawford, the Congregationalist missionary, arrived in the gulch in early 1863, he wrote back that "[t]able board is now eight dollars a week. Flour is $15.00 a sack, that is $30.00 a barrel; butter 75 to 85 cents per pound; eggs $1.50 per dozen; potatoes 12 1/2 cents per pound; milk 30 cents per quart; hay $120 to $125 per ton; and other things in proportion. Interest is from five to fifteen per cent a month. You will see it is rather hard to live if one has money, and very hard if one has not."[38]

Clara, who was already acquiring property in the early 1860's, was faced with interest rates that were only slightly less usurious. She purchased 2 building lots on the south side of Lawrence Street in Central City on a deed of trust, for $500; Henry Teller, later U.S. Senator but already a prominent local attorney, apparently held the deed. The lots were described as "bounded on the east by the Episcopal Chapel."[39] The interest rate was 3% a month.

Supplies she would have needed for her laundry would have also come dear. Before the railroad came to the area in 1872, firewood was the fuel of choice for firing boilers such as she would have used, and firewood was in short supply indeed.

Plunging into the seemingly endless forests of the Rocky Mountains, the earliest miners were heedless of the dangers of wildfires. As seen above, Reverend Goode wrote that on the road to the diggings the travelers were "coal-blackened by the late mountain fires."[40] As early as June of that first year, 1859, "a destructive fire broke out and raged above the Jackson Diggings, which burned three men. Their remains were subsequently found, but they were never identified."[41] Even such a Colorado booster as the *Rocky Mountain News'* William Byers admitted that, by 1870, "one-third to one-half of Colorado's forests had been destroyed by fire in the past decade."[42]

Nor were the fires confined to the mountain forests. Nevadaville, the rough-and-ready mining town just up Nevada Gulch from Central City, was devastated by a fire in November of 1860. But despite the ravages of the flames, the real despoiler of the timberlands was, as Duane Smith observed, the miner himself. Wood was essential for building homes, timbering mineshafts, constructing windlasses and hoists, as well as for burning to power the area's innumerable boilers and engines. As early as the mid-1860s, Hollister wrote that few trees "now remain within five or six miles around."[43] By the '70s, a local newspaper estimated that "Gilpin County used 100,000 cords of wood per annum, which cost $6 per cord in summer, $9 and $10 in winter, plus $2.50 for the man who cut it up."[44] Samuel Cushman put the price in 1864 at $12 per cord.[45]

With the hills for miles around denuded of trees, floods in the narrow valley were a frequent occurrence, with Black Hawk, at the mouth of the gulch where it poured into Clear Creek, the usual site of the worst destruction. Otherwise, though, drinkable water was in almost as short supply as firewood, with both being used—and wasted—in absurd quantities by the mills in Black Hawk. Bela Buell's stamp mill in Central City, for example, "had access to 20,000 gallons of water but 200,000 were needed daily to operate his properties. The same water had to be used repeatedly. Therefore, he built a series of settling tanks with a total capacity of 500,000 gallons to cleanse the water for reuse in the mill."[46]

As a result, the supply for individual residents was limited, at best. Cushman wrote that the local water situation, "owing to the scarcity of good wells, is unique. The peripatetic water vendor, and owner of some fine springs in the upper part of the city, goes around with an iron tank holding ten barrels, and through a hose leading from tank to kitchen, pumps up or discharges downward, as the case may be, a barrel or two at the tune of *thirty-five cents per barrel!*"[47] If Clara was forced to buy water from these itinerant peddlers, her costs for laundry services were severely impacted.

Besides fires and floods, there were other dangers. Sanitation was virtually non-existent; the gulch itself was the sewer system for the towns along it for most of the century. The mines and mills were either drafty or unventilated. Consequently, diseases were frequent and deadly. As early as 1863, Reverend Crawford wrote that a "reliable physician in Central City tells me that there have been more cases of lung disease this last spring than he ever knew elsewhere, five to one.... Rheumatism is common in the mountains and fever and erysipelas both here and in Denver."[48] A later writer noted that "life in Central City was...a world debilitated by intestinal and respiratory illnesses...."[49]

Several of the diaries recorded the health woes of the early miners, as one who wrote, "I was making money rapidly, when in the Fall I was taken sick with the mountain fever...."[50] And accidents in the mines and mills were a constant threat.

Physicians were by no means in short supply in the gulch from the earliest days; one of Green Russell's brothers was a doctor, as was a member of Gregory's party. There were so many that Reverend Goode reported that "[s]igns of 'Dr.' stick out from cabins, shanties, tents, and wagons, and the title is heard in almost every company in the diggings."[51]

But, perhaps because of economic factors, not all the medical men in the gulch towns prospered. "Despite the variety of illnesses, Dr. William Grafton found too few patients to satisfy his practice and had moved...from Nevada to Central to Denver."[52]

Perhaps Grafton's problem was more a lack of payments than of patients. Certainly a number of physicians supported themselves in the area. But Clara, whether through training or disposition, still found her services much in demand. An 1890 *Denver Republican* article remembered that "[s]he was always the first to nurse a sick miner or the wife of one,"[53] and at her death it was eulogized that she "smoothed the pillow and answered the appeal for help of many a poor sufferer in the days that tried the truest hearts."[54]

So it seems that, by the early 1860s, Clara had become an important and respected part of the pioneer community in Gilpin County. A single businesswoman, she prospered in spite of the scarcity of the basic supplies that she needed to practice her trade. She was valued for her ability to provide basic medical care, or at least comfort for the ill and injured of that community. And she continued to support, financially and otherwise, a number of the fledgling churches that were helping to provide at least a veneer of civilization, culture and Christianity to the rapidly growing mining camps.

Given her beginnings in slavery, her age when she came to the camps, and her success in spite of her second-class status as an African-American woman, Clara's story to this point would have already been worthy of our admiration, if not our amazement. But the most remarkable part of her saga still lay in the future.

Chapter 6

Aunt Clara's hard work as a laundress, supplemented perhaps by fees or gifts she might have received for her medical care (including, as the area became home to more married couples, as a midwife), would have eventually gained her a comfortable, if hard-earned, standard of living. But Clara achieved a level of prosperity, even of wealth, quite in excess of what she could have earned through her laundering, even considering "the unusual returns of a mining camp for labor such as hers."[1] In fact, right after quoting Clara's prices for laundering shirts, Burrell wrote that in "a few years she had accumulated property valued at about $10,000."[2]

The *Republican* detailed her accomplishments further, writing that after settling in Central City, Clara "added still further to the store of her worldly goods. As the years rolled by she invested her surplus money in real estate, and in 1864 she was the owner of seven good houses in Central City, sixteen lots in Denver and some good property in Georgetown and Boulder."[3] Investments such as these would have yielded a substantial income; as Duane Smith observed, in the Civil War years of the early 1860's, "Central Citians…fussed about high rents; buildings on the main streets cost $300-400 and houses $100-175 per month."[4] Using those figures, Clara could at times have been earning over $1000 a month from her Central City properties alone!

So well known was Aunt Clara as a landowner that she was used as an example in current political arguments. During a dispute regarding the valuation for tax purposes of the Central City bank of Thatcher, Standley & Company, a letter was printed in the *Daily Central City Register* from one signing himself as "A Cornish Tax Payer:"

> It has frequently been said that this is a great country for the industrious poor to get rich in, and our city is a good illustration of this. By this book we find that Aunt Clara, who, a few years ago, was a slave, (if we mistake not, in Mr. Thatcher's native State), has, by honest industry at the washtub, accumulated so much property that its assessed value is greater than that of the institution above referred to.…[5]

Though sometimes portrayed as a naïve, almost ignorant ex-slave, everything in her life demonstrated that Clara combined the virtues of Christian charity with a shrewd business sense. Even so, however, we must conclude that to build a real estate empire of this sort, she would have needed some assistance.

For one thing, as was seen earlier, even if her working schedule would have permitted it, public transportation would still have been unavailable to Clara as a black woman. Viewing houses and lots over such a wide area in the early 1860's would have been extremely time-consuming. And correspondence describing the properties would have been of little help, as it is believed that Clara was illiterate.

Distressing though this assertion is, it is supported by all the accounts we have of Clara, and verified by some of her recorded property transactions. James Thomson, the English poet who shared a six-hour stagecoach ride with Clara some years later, noted in his diary that Clara "can't read or write...."[6] Her signature never appears on any of the property transactions of hers that are recorded, and on one, an 1868 sale of 400 feet of the Argentine lode, recorded in Clear Creek County Record Book Z, p. 718, notation is made that Clara signed with an "X". Most of the Gilpin County deeds show "her mark," and many bear indications such as one from 1868, in which note is made that "in the presence of James Burrell witness of Clara Brown by her mark."[7]

Certainly, if Clara had been taught to read or write, she would have been the exception to the rule. Though apparently she was treated kindly by her masters back in Kentucky, and the practice of slavery was perhaps less harshly implemented there than elsewhere, there was still a prevailing distrust of giving slaves the power of literacy. As Coleman wrote in *Slavery Times in Kentucky*:

> *Although there was never any law passed in Kentucky, which prohibited teaching slaves to read and write, public sentiment operated strongly against it. Many of the slave owners were willing that their slaves be taught to read the Bible; yet there was the constant dread of their reading "filthy abolitionist literature," tending to promote insubordination, an overt uprising, or make them thoroughly dissatisfied with their lot. Also, it was believed that, by the slaves becoming able to read or write, it would be easy for them to forge "free papers" or passes for themselves, and others of their kind.[8]*

So with the background of those limitations upon Clara's ability to seek out and wisely invest in properties—and judging from her results, she invested very wisely indeed—we can naturally ask how, then, she managed to buy and sell such scattered properties so profitably.

The answer probably lies in her role, only hinted at in some of the contemporaneous biographical accounts, as a sort of mother figure to the rapidly growing African-American community in Colorado. There were 46 black residents of the area identified in the 1860 census, but just 10 years later, the number residing in the Territory had jumped nearly ten-fold, to 456.[9] As one of the first blacks to arrive in the Pikes Peak country, as one of the few black women, and certainly as the eldest black woman in Colorado, she would have earned a considerable degree of deference and consideration from the younger black males who gradually made their way to the Rockies. Over the remaining years of her life in Central City, and even continuing in her declining years in Denver, there is evidence of Clara's contact with a number of black miners and merchants, many of whom were themselves heavily involved in trading residential, commercial and mining properties throughout Colorado.

The first and best known of these was Barney Launcelot Ford. With Ford, as with Clara herself and so many former slaves, precise family information is hard to come by.[10] Bruyn, writing her biography of Aunt Clara in 1970, relied heavily on Forbes Parkhill's biography of Ford. Unfortunately, Parkhill was as prone to dramatization as Bruyn herself.[11] Still, the basic outline of Ford's life is clear enough.

Unlike Clara, Ford somehow learned to read and write. He escaped from his master, and with the help of the Underground Railroad, fled to Chicago. There he met Henry Wagoner, who would later join him in Colorado, and married Wagoner's sister-in-law, Julia Lyoni.

Ford was early bitten by the gold bug—one account says that he worked as a teenager in the Georgia gold fields[12]—and sailed for the California gold fields in 1848. But on the overland voyage across the isthmus of Nicaragua, Ford decided that opening a hotel serving his fellow travelers there would be more lucrative than mining in California. He was probably right, as despite numerous adventures (including at one point working for Commodore Vanderbilt) he returned to Chicago a wealthy man. He opened a livery stable, which doubled as a station of the Underground Railroad, and prospered still further.

With the news of John Gregory's discoveries in Colorado, Ford was smitten with gold fever again. But arriving in Colorado in 1860, he found that most of the best land around the original find was long since claimed. He also found that the West was not the land of equal opportunity some had proclaimed; unable to find a room to rent when he arrived in Mountain City, he was referred to Aunt Clara, who gladly took him in. He filed two claims, but both were "jumped" by white miners.

Whether in spite of or because of Aunt Clara's advice, Ford decided to go across the continental divide to mine the Blue River country near today's Breckenridge. He had by then linked up with some other black miners, but "they found a strong sentiment against them and, drifting together for self-protection, took up placer ground in French Gulch, which has proved to be very profitable."[13] Again, though, his claims were "jumped" by white prospectors.

Cured of gold fever, Ford returned to Denver. He opened a successful barbershop, but it (along with much of downtown Denver) was destroyed by fire in April, 1863. With a $9,000 loan from banker Luther Kountze—at 25% annual interest!—Ford opened the People's Restaurant in August. It was an immediate hit—it had a bar upstairs and a "shaving and hairdressing saloon" in the basement.

Paying back Kountze's loan in just 90 days, Ford soon opened restaurants and hotels in Denver, Breckenridge, Cheyenne and even San Francisco. His crowning accomplishments were the Inter-Ocean Hotels in Denver and Cheyenne, the latter built for $65,000 and fine enough to host President Ulysses

S. Grant.

With Ford's success as a restaurateur, hotelier and developer in Denver, he could well have steered Clara toward some of the purchases of lots and houses she made there. But much of Clara's fortune came from her trading in interests in mining claims in Gilpin and adjacent Clear Creek counties. Given Ford's spotty record as a mining entrepreneur, Clara must have had better advisers than he in this sort of transaction. Fortunately, she knew two of the best.

Jeremiah Lee and Lorenzo Bowman were partners in several enterprises, though each had individual mining holdings of his own, as well. Bowman is the lesser-known figure today, perhaps because of his premature death in 1870.

Lee, on the other hand, lived in Central City until his death in 1904. By that time he was greatly respected as "the pioneer colored man of Colorado,"[14] and the events of his life were outlined in considerable detail. One such biographical sketch, written by Georgetown newspaperman Jesse Randall in 1903, was apparently seen by Lee himself,[15] who seems to have vouched for its accuracy.

Unlike Clara, Barney Ford, and most of the early black residents of Colorado, Lee seems to have spent little or no time in slavery.[16] Randall reported that he was born in 1829 in what became West Virginia, but that "at the age of twelve his parents moved to Illinois and then to Missouri."

He served with the army in the Mexican War, taking part in the battles of El Paso and Sacramento (in Chihuahua). Though he was permanently deafened by the cannon fire, his service was never officially recognized—he might have been too young to formally enlist. After returning briefly to his parents, he was a victim of the California gold fever, and set off overland in 1850. He stayed there for four years, returning east by ship.

He was married, probably during this period, but "in 1859 he caught the gold fever and came to Colorado, making his headquarters at Central City, and spent the first three years prospecting in every direction, before, he says, he became satisfied it was a country fit, even for a wolf, to live in." It's likely that he made the acquaintance of Aunt Clara at this time, especially as he was separated from his wife, Emily, and children. He must have been a devoted family man, as Randall noted that he "crossed the plains nine times before a railroad was built. And in 1863, brought his family out from Missouri."

Randall said that Lee "acquired considerable mining property in Gilpin county," so he may well have been a source for the information Clara used for some of her purchases at this time.

Lee made several discoveries and claims in cooperation with Lorenzo Bowman, whom Randall called his "companion prospector." As Randall wrote, "Bowman was called 'Professor' for the reason that he was the only person here who knew anything about smelting ore, having been employed in the lead smelters of Missouri,"[17] which may be where he met Lee.

An account of Bowman's early expertise in the field of smelting ore is mixed with admiration for his accomplishments and scorn for his race. At least three different versions of the story exist; the most concise and useful comes from the Central City paper. Caleb Stowell had transported a Scotch hearth furnace for smelting ore—lead, at first—from Galena, Illinois. But, as the *Register* reported:

> We understand that Mr. Stowell's Scotch hearth is at length turning out lead very finely. The proprietors and several other persons attempted to get it to work well, at length they secured the services of Mr. Bowman, one of our colored citizens, who succeeded at once. In consideration of his success the citizens of Georgetown have conferred on him the title of Professor.[18]

Typically, Bowman's prospecting investments were small in scale; he sold a number of discovery claims in Gilpin County for amounts for $10 to $250 in the period from December, 1863 to May, 1865. But occasionally, a claim would prove more lucrative, as when in April, 1866, he sold a claim on the Motley lode in the Illinois Central mining district.[19] A New York attorney, P.S. Sherry, handled the sale, which netted $2000 for Bowman. But the sale also yielded $1000 each for Clara (through her attorney, Willard Teller, Henry's brother), Sarah and Alice Lee (two of Jeremiah Lee's daughters), and a number of prominent white investors, including Bela Buell and Central City businessman Samuel J. Lorah.

Later, Lee and Bowman built the Red, White and Blue smelter in Leavenworth Gulch, and also "the first road over Burrell hill, a road that was in use for many years, over which millions of dollars worth of ore was hauled."[20] By this time, their operations were largely in Clear Creek County, where Bowman chiefly resided; although he had purchased residential property in Central City, it seems to have been for investment purposes.[21] Taken as a whole, Clara's transactions with Bowman were probably the most lucrative of her many investments. It is likely no coincidence that her fortunes began to founder after his death.

Lee continued to live in Central City. As members of what was probably the largest, and surely the wealthiest, black family in Central (an article in the *Chicago Daily News*, March 18, 1890, on Colorado's "Men of Color" estimated his wealth at $40-50,000), the Lees would undoubtedly have been in regular and close contact with Clara.

Whether Clara received information from Lee, Bowman, or others, as early as 1862 she was buying residential property in "Payne's Bar," a section of what later became Idaho Springs, in Clear Creek County. She purchased a mining claim from early Gilpin sheriff William "Jack" Kehler as early as August, 1860. Over the years, she was persistent and prudent in her acquisitions. As noted above, by 1864 she had put together a substantial real estate empire, and a fortune estimated at $10,000.

But Aunt Clara was not one for acquiring wealth for its own sake. She had already laid up "treasures in heaven," a reward she was confident of realizing one day. Rather, she saw wealth as a necessity toward continuing the search for her long-lost daughter, Eliza Jane. And if other opportunities to help out her black brothers and sisters came along, she would be ready to assist.

Chapter 7

While Clara and the black miners and merchants of Colorado were prospering, however, the rest of the country was suffering, and particularly so were their fellow African-Americans. The Civil War left Colorado generally untouched (Chivington's battle of Glorietta Pass was fought with Colorado regulars and volunteers, but took place in New Mexico), but "the States" back east were ravaged.

As opposed to the conditions in the east, however, the Colorado mining towns were merely struggling. Black Hawk and Central City had been formally incorporated in 1864, which added a new layer of legitimacy to the territorial and county government that had succeeded the earliest miner's courts. Building was still going on, and immigration continued.

But the area's principal industry—mining and milling—had been racked with a series of reverses, some of which were inherent to the industry, some of which were caused—or at least exacerbated—by events further east.

As seen above in the letters from as early as 1859, the mining industry had moved away from the comparatively easy, inexpensive and profitable gulch mining—hydraulic mining that removed the surface gold with little effort—toward deep rock mining, tunneling into the mountains to follow a vein of ore, ore that would then have to be processed to yield gold in a acceptably pure form. And certainly gulch mining continued for the next few years, while the initial methods of processing the lode gold—largely stamp milling, at that point—were producing increasing amounts of wealth. Cushman summarized the developments:

> The year 1862 brought a more hopeful feeling among the lode miners. Several prominent mines…were now producing better than ever. The mines were from 100 to 200 feet deep, and no one questioned their permanence…. The premium on gold rising more rapidly than prices of labor and supplies, further stimulated activity. The mill process was now generally understood, and the gulch mines still gave employment to hundreds of miners.
>
> On the other hand, there were ores shown to be rich by assay, from which the stamp process would extract but little gold. The increasing depths of the mines made steam power indispensable. The water was increasing. Unskillful timbering must be renewed, and shafts must be straightened for permanent work. These things did not diminish faith in mining, but began to be talked of as evidence that "poor men have no business to pursue mining."[1]

This need for additional capital coincided with two other developments that nearly ruined the Colorado mining industry. On the one hand, companies began erecting larger and larger stamp mills, "several of them purchasing stamp mills with all accompanying machinery capable of crushing from fifty to one hundred tons of ore per day."[2] But the ores were proving increasingly difficult to treat with such a crude method. The 1880 *History of Clear Creek and Boulder Valleys* put it this way: "Rich ores were treated only to be ruined. The precious metals could not be extracted and separated from the mass of worthless materials. The tailings and refuse of the mills were more valuable than what was saved from them."[3]

Smelters, such as Lee & Bowman's Red, White and Blue smelter in Leavenworth Gulch, proved useful, but were still inefficient and limited in capacity. Cushman continued: "Another cause of failure, was the absence of smelting works or any other reduction works, for the suitable treatment of the richest portion of the ore. This brought upon us a horde of PROCESS MEN. Indeed, the plague began in 1863, and lasted as long as there was money around to be wasted."[4]

The "processes" were pseudo-scientific mixtures of common sense, known treatments and alchemical chimeras, developed by miners and promoters desperate for ways to release the gold trapped in the quartz rock. Keith desulphurizers, Crosby & Thompson roasting cylinders, Bertola pans, the Mason steamer, the Monnier Metallurgical Process—all claimed astounding rates of return, but distracted attention from legitimate smelting experiments, like Lee & Bowman's, or a new smelter just below Black Hawk erected by James E. Lyon.

The process mania was scorned by those who looked back like Cushman, writing in 1876. But to those present at the time, like Congregationalist missionary William Crawford, it seemed in early 1864 to be the very salvation of the industry: "Large stock companies formed in the East will commence operations in the spring and with processes far superior to those hitherto employed. Probably four times as much gold will be saved as heretofore, at the same expense."[5]

The need for capital to invest in such spurious processes simply accelerated a trend toward reliance on eastern investment. New York and Boston capitalists, watching their investments at home shrink with the rampant inflation fueled by the ongoing Civil War, sought ever more lucrative returns, and the Colorado miners were happy to accept their money. Nor did the speculators limit themselves to investments in mills and smelters. Even interests in the mines themselves were offered up for sale.

> *During this time nearly all the developed mining property in the county, and a much larger amount of wholly undeveloped claims—bonded by the score without reference to contiguity—sold ten thousand times higher in proportion to their value. It appeared that the Eastern promoters wanted anything upon which stock might be issued; the people wanted*

*anything in exchange for the rapidly depreciating greenbacks;
and the mine-owners—well, they were not afraid of greenbacks, providing the pile was large enough.*[6]

The litany of the wildly inflated sales is a lengthy one, and countless examples of the ridiculous prices paid could be cited. In October, 1863, "a group of New Yorkers paid nearly $200,000 for approximately 460 feet of gold-bearing ground"[7] called the Ophir mine, discovered by legendary Irish miner Pat Casey; some investors paid $2,000 per foot on the Gregory.[8] Just as the Panic of 1857 combined with the rumors of gold discoveries to lure 100,000 men to the Pikes Peak region, the dire Civil War economy and inflation of 1863-4 combined with the rumors of fabulous profits to be made in gold mines to lure millions of eastern dollars into the Gilpin County mines and mills. As Hollister later wrote:

*There is no necessity for a history in detail of the
transfer of the quartz-mines of Colorado to Eastern men. It is
sufficient to say that a mania for Colorado mining property
was created in New York and Boston about the end of 1863,
and fabulous prices,—in several cases a thousand dollars a
foot, were given for improved mines. Surely that was tempta-
tion enough; we need look no further for the causes of the
mania for selling out which responded in Colorado to the
mania for buying in the East.*[9]

For those with mining properties to sell—and that included Lee and Bowman, and probably by now Aunt Clara herself—such conditions were obviously favorable. Some miners, such as the Briggs brothers of Central City, "sold their mine to New Yorkers in 1864 and watched as the new owners poured more than $50,000 into developing and improving the property, only to abandon it four years later as a result of the high costs. Seeing a fresh opportunity, the Briggs brothers repurchased the mine at a sheriff's sale (for much less than they sold it) and quickly had it producing again, helping them to purchase neighboring mines and add to a growing list of investments."[10] And with established lodes selling for such ludicrous prices, the search was on for new properties to sell. Reverend Crawford wrote in April of 1864:

*The fever of speculation now runs very high. A large
amount of mining property is bonded for sale in the New York
market, and a large amount has already been sold. The mountains have been prospected anew, and many very rich lodes
discovered. The recorder's office is crowded every day by those
who are entering new claims, and looking up their old, and
hitherto, worthless, property. How long the excitement will
continue it is impossible to say. The mines are so rich and
extensive, and so much capital has already been invested, that
we do not look for any serious and damaging reaction, such as
has occurred in the history of most of the western states.*[11]

Unfortunately, Reverend Crawford was no better a prognosticator than he was a mining engineer. The buying frenzy was peaking by late 1863, by which time the sheer volume of deals threatened to overload the county's legal framework: "By the end of 1863, it was a weekly occurrence to add a new recording clerk to the office force. Work went on twenty-four hours a day as clerks recorded and filed the various legal instruments necessary to secure titles to mining property. Telegraph lines had reached Central City by November 7, 1863, and telegrams about mining deals made the wires hum between New York and Central City. Many of these telegrams cost between $50.00 and $350.00 each."[12] Gilpin County Clerk and Recorder Bela Buell had the second highest wage in the territory, at $40,000, trailing only new territorial Governor John Evans.[13]

But the very telegraph that made purchases so simple also made the investors better able to inform themselves on the actual condition of their mining investments. Even the *Daily Mining Journal*, April 5, 1864, recognized the dangers: "Those who have the true interest of Colorado at heart, will uniformly frown on all attempts to swindle parties in the East by selling at enormous figures property which has no known existence, outside the Recorder's office.... Never in the history of the country did the excitement of mining speculation run so high as at present. Men are every day receiving windfalls in the shape of receipts from the sales of claims to Eastern capitalists....[the] state of things is unhealthy...."[14]

Many of the eastern companies had dispatched managers to their mining properties, but few were remotely qualified: "jolly dogs" Cushman called them, in a scathing indictment of their incompetence.[15] But some were quite capable, and soon saw the real "value" of their companies' holdings. The more accurate reporting soon caused the bubble to burst.

> *The end came rather suddenly on April 21, 1864, when news of a 'miniature panic' on Wall Street was circulated in Central City. The warning came in the form of telegrams by New York speculators to their representatives in Gilpin. At noon that day, the Recorder's office had been packed with speculators, all filing claims about which they knew nothing but for which they were asking exorbitant prices. The dispatches telling of the crisis in New York arrived at one o'clock; the news was circulated among the crowd "and lo: the office was deserted as quickly as if a case of Cholera were troubling them."*[16]

Still, the speculation had produced spectacular profits for some, and Clara may well have been among them. Some, like Pat Casey, took their money and ran. Casey ran all the way to New York, where he "plunged into a successful business in stock and gold speculation,"[17] traveling to his appointments in one of the city's most luxurious coaches with a jet-black team, which he extravagantly valued at $2,500.

But for those who remained—like Clara, like Bowman and Lee—times were, if not exactly hard, not quite so exuberant. Certainly fortunes had been lost, as well as made, and the effects could be clearly seen. A reporter from *Harper's Monthly Magazine* visited the towns, and found many mills and other reductions works "as silent as the tomb. Scattered in all directions around half-finished, roofless buildings can be seen boilers and engines, stamps and crushers, pans and amalgamators, and machinery of every kind, half buried in the soil, rusting and wasting, lying in the roads, even driven over by the traveler as he passes the wreck—a monument of one kind of Eastern mining."[18]

The mining slump—gold production slipped from $1.7 million in 1864 to $1.45 million in 1865, and just $725 thousand a year later—depressed workers' salaries initially, while "Indian trouble" interfered with freighting across the plains and actually drove the already high prices up. "These tribulations generated more strife and a restless May 1864 for Gilpin County, including several wildcat strikes. Management won that particular round and another one in October, protesting heatedly that raising wages would be suicidal to continuing operations. Wages nonetheless increased from July's $4.00 to $4.25, to February's $5.00 to $5.50. Paid in inflated greenbacks, miners knew they were not coming out ahead."[19]

Still, compared to the residents of the devastated eastern states, the workingmen—and women—of Colorado were far better off. Besides whatever profit Clara was making on her property and mining investments—she had paid $350 for some mining claims on Illinois Bar, near Idaho Springs, in 1863, for example—her laundry business was continuing to thrive, as well.

The combination of the economic conditions that prevailed in the country and the mining towns, and the new freedom of transportation that Clara and other blacks would have enjoyed as a result of the end of the Civil War and the abolition of slavery, presented Clara with an opportunity to put her new wealth to use. Sometime during the summer of 1865, she made up her mind to return to the states.

Her purpose seems to have been two-fold. First, she intended to search through the carnage and chaos of Kentucky and Tennessee for any word of her missing daughter, Eliza Jane. And second, failing to find 'Liza Jane or her family, Clara thought to utilize some of her good fortune to help some of her fellow blacks to emigrate to Colorado to begin new lives.

Chapter 8

That Clara chose to return to Kentucky and Tennessee, rather than take her efforts to the Deep South, reinforces that her primary motive was to search for 'Liza Jane, rather than to resettle newly freed slaves. But certainly the level of misery there, if not perhaps as graphic as that in other parts of the former slave states, was nonetheless profound.

The situation in the Border States like Kentucky and Tennessee was somewhat confused throughout the war. A politically divided Tennessee was the last state to secede from the Union, but in large part fell under Union control early in the war—Nashville was taken by Union troops on February 24, 1862 and Memphis on June 6. Under former governor Andrew Johnson, military government replaced the civilian one for the duration of the conflict. But the control was tentative, with continued outbreaks of violent retribution by one side or the other, and ongoing pitched battles in East Tennessee. A diary kept by a 16-year-old Southern sympathizer in Gallatin has the telling entry on April 28th, 1864, "[r]emarkably quiet; no murdering for several days."

Even with goodwill on both sides, the situation would have been grim. The economic system had completely collapsed, and "the Valley of the Tennessee had been laid waste."[1] Much of the devastation came not from the war itself, but from the provisioning of both Union and Confederate armies throughout the state at various times during the conflict. "Anything of value that could be eaten or carried off was taken by soldiers of both sides," it is written in Tennessee's official history, the "Blue Book." "Tennessee's unfortunate position as the breadbasket for two different armies…brought more destruction and loss of property than was caused by actual combat."

Farm production and property values would not reach their 1860 levels again until 1900. Hundreds of households were without men; former slaves—and at the time of emancipation there were approximately 275,000 of them—had now to deal with former slave owners as wage earners, but no one had money to hire. Many of the ex-slaves were homeless and destitute. Black laborers were impressed from military "contraband" camps to build the federal military infrastructure. In late 1863, the Union army began mustering in all-black regiments; ultimately, 20,133 black troops would serve, providing fully 40 percent of the Tennessee contingent to the Union forces. But when the troops were mustered out at war's end, they faced an uncertain future in a beaten and bloodied society.

Though Kentucky was nominally a Union state, its predicament was not much different than Tennessee's. In fact, 63 counties did secede, setting up a Confederate government in Bowling Green. More than 30,000 Kentuckians went south to fight for the Confederacy; 60,000 joined the Union army, including 20,000 blacks—some of whom were conscripted, beginning in 1864. Reflecting the state's ambivalence, both Abraham Lincoln and the Confederate president, Jefferson Davis, were native Kentuckians.

The state was likewise a military crossroads, with different sections held by different armies at different times throughout the war. More military actions—453—took place in Kentucky than in many southern states, such as Alabama, Maryland, or either of the Carolinas. But the ultimate fate of the state's allegiance was decided at the battle of Perryville, where 4,211 Union and 3,396 Confederate soldiers died in a standoff that preserved the state for the Union cause.

Moreover—ironically—slaveholding was legal until 1865 in Kentucky. Lincoln's Emancipation Proclamation of 1863 freed only the slaves in the rebel states; not until the passage of the Thirteenth Amendment, after the end of the War,[2] were those slaves still held in the northern states deemed free. Surviving slaveholders bitterly resisted any federal "interference" in the horrid custom. Practically, however, the slaveholding society of the prewar days had ended; but nothing had emerged to take its place. Worse still, the beginnings of the white backlash against the freed slaves had already begun; the Ku Klux Klan was formed not in the 1870's in the Deep South, but in 1865 in Pulaski, Tennessee.[3] In many ways, in fact, African-Americans were worse off in the Border States than elsewhere. For one thing, there were few free blacks prior to emancipation to provide both role models and a support system for the newly freed slaves. In 1860, just 4.5% of Kentucky's black residents were free, and just 2.6% of Tennessee's. This ratio seems more like that of cotton belt states like South Carolina (2.4%) or Louisiana (5.3%) than other northern slave states like Maryland (49.1%) or even Virginia (10.6%).[4]

The accounts of Clara's journey back east are sketchy and contradictory; while she was doubtless well-known in the African-American community in Colorado, and widely respected in the Christian community as well, she had not yet begun to receive the widespread recognition in the general population that she would in later years. Still, her journey was sufficiently newsworthy to rate considerable notice in the state's pre-eminent newspaper, William Byers' *Rocky Mountain News*. An article in the August 7, 1866 issue was headed "A Woman in a Thousand."

> *Mrs. Clara Brown, (colored) better known to old Coloradians as "Aunt Clara," came here in '59, and by dint of hard labor and perseverance had amassed quite a fortune. Last October the secret of her economy and industry for all these years came to light, and her object apparent. She at that time went east and has since devoted her time and energies to looking up her numerous progeny; for that purpose she traveled*

through the length and breadth of Kentucky and Tennessee, gathering together her flock, and the result is she has now come back to her chosen home in the mountains, with her sons and daughters, with their husbands and wives, and their children, sixteen in all. She brought them all out at her own expense, arriving last week, and proposes to settle them around her, where she can have an eye upon their movements and future welfare. We will put "Aunt Clara" against the world, white or black, for industry, perseverance, mercy and filial love.[5]

Among the standard biographical sources, Burrell's account is the most detailed, but it differs from the *News* article in several particulars:

At the close of the war, she went to her old Kentucky home, and hunted up all her relatives that could be found, thirty-four in number, and brought them to Leavenworth by steamboat, and then purchased a train, crossed the plains, and settled her relatives in Denver, Central City and Georgetown.[6]

Thomson's diary entry is shorter, but still useful.

After the war went to Tennessee, where she was raised, and gathered together and brought out here twenty-six relatives and orphans, at a cost of $4000.[7]

The geographical confusion is pretty easily explained: Logan County, where Clara served most of her years in slavery, is in western Kentucky, bordering the Tennessee line. Sumner County, Tennessee, of which Gallatin is the county seat, is just over the state line to the southeast. It's not unlikely, if she was indeed searching for her missing 'Liza Jane, that Clara would have traveled to several counties in her search, even over "the length and breadth" of the two states, as the *News* put it. Interestingly, just after the description of this trip, the *Republican* adds that "[a]bout this time Aunt Clara offered $1,000 reward for the discovery of her lost daughter, Eliza Jane, and she caused letters of inquiry to be sent all over the country."[8] Considering the nearly ruinous effect the trip had upon her finances, it seems likely that this reward would have been offered before her trip, and that she was traveling in the Kentucky-Tennessee area to broadcast it as widely as she could.

But if Clara was attempting to find Eliza, her efforts were futile. This leads one to wonder if the *News* account of her motivation was a later justification. Given what we know of Clara's kindness and merciful disposition, might it not be that a trip that began as an effort to locate her daughter became, once that purpose proved fruitless, a rescue mission? Certainly Hall's account, written a few years after Clara's death, makes it sound as though her entire purpose in her work and investments was to "accumulate funds for the execution of the great purpose of her life, which was to find and rescue her children from bondage...."[9]

We'll never know for sure Aunt Clara's thinking in making this trip.

But if she saw it as primarily a search for her lost daughter, it might explain the apparent lack of preparation for bringing back such a large number of fellow blacks that led to the financial disaster she faced. The *Republican* wrote that a "white man who was associated with the enterprise turned out to be not as honest as she thought him, and she was out of pocket about $4000 before the emigrants landed in Colorado."[10] This is, as noted, the cost of the journey that was recorded by Thomson, though he did so without any indication that he thought the price was exorbitant. Of course, he was an Englishman, newly arrived in the country, and unfamiliar with distances or prices. More importantly, he was writing in a personal journal that he intended primarily for his own recollections; he may well have been more impressed that this elderly ex-slave would have had $4000 to spend!

Since two of the four contemporaneous accounts indicate that Clara brought twenty-six persons with her, and that they traveled by rail to Leavenworth (Burrell's suggestion that they came there by steamboat makes little sense), we can pretty well establish the costs for that part of the journey. Kathleen Bruyn, in her research for her book-length biography of Aunt Clara, had extensive contact with officials of the Louisville & Nashville Railroad.

The pre-war burst of railroad building had left the eastern United States crisscrossed with a spider web of small rail lines, and the L&N's Charles Castner put together an itinerary that involved five different railroads, passing through five states. Castner figured the distance on this route to be just over 700 miles, and the average cost per mile to be five cents; that yields a one-way fare from Russellville to Leavenworth of $35.[11] So this part of the trip would have cost Clara's entourage just under $1000 for a group of 26.

The trip would have been much simpler and quicker than Clara's first trip west from Kentucky—that one was probably made largely by riverboat—but reminders of the earlier journey would have remained. Castner suggested that, even though the war was over, "the party would have been 'segregated' or seated in a separate coach on southern lines...a practice that appears to have been followed even before the later 'Jim Crow' laws and 'partitioned' coaches for the two races."[12] Still, considering how Clara would have had to travel in the antebellum years, this journey must have seemed a triumphant return.

By this time, wagon trains from Leavenworth to Denver crossed the plains on a regular basis. But unlike the stagecoaches, that had posted arrival and departure times and fixed fares, the composition of the trains varied according to the travelers, their equipment and supplies. If Clara "purchased a train," as Burrell put it, she could well have been victimized by an unscrupulous wagonmaster at this point. Assuming most of her charges were young families, able to walk alongside the wagons, and they had few personal belongings, the train could have been relatively small and lightly provisioned. That being the case, a cost of $3000 for crossing the plains would have been wildly out of line.

The newly freed slaves, of course, would have had no idea what a proper cost would be; the whole trip would have been like entering an entirely new world for them. And Clara's recollections of her own passage six years earlier would have been of little help; she worked for her fare that time. So the possibility of exploitation in this part of the journey is very likely.

But whether or not Clara was cheated in this transaction, she and her company eventually made their way to Colorado. Amazingly enough, there seems to have been a witness to Clara's trip across the plains. Mrs. Eliza Smith Gilmore, "daughter of free colored parents of Cleveland, Ohio," was interviewed for a booklet on the state's ethnic diversity, published by the Colorado State Department of Education, in 1961.

> *We went from Kansas City to a small freighting town in Kansas, where mother bought a team of mules and supplies, hired a driver, and received information that a party of covered wagons was just a day ahead of us, and as they were drawn by oxen and our wagon by mules, we could overtake them. We did, and it was there we met Aunt Clara Brown, who was bringing her covered wagon with emancipated slaves, at her own expense, from Leavenworth, Kansas, back to Central City, Colorado. They brought twenty or thirty people at a time.* [13]

But before we examine the details of the settlement of these "emancipated slaves" in such startlingly different surroundings, we need first to ask: who were these people?

Here again the accounts differ significantly. The *News* article, written nearest the event, calls the emigrants "her numerous progeny," and details further "her sons and daughters, with their husbands and wives, and their children, sixteen in all." But as seen earlier, the *Republican* article had that "[s]ome of them were friends and acquaintances, but the majority were orphans who had no home." Thomson recorded that the emigrants were "relatives and orphans," while Burrell mentioned simply "relatives."

Bruyn dismissed the *News* account, writing in her notes that "obviously the relationships whole-cloth."[14] And considering what we later know of Aunt Clara, and her tireless search for her missing daughter, an article that has her arriving in Colorado with her "sons and daughters" makes very little sense.

We can at least guess a reason for the confusion. The *News* reporter— very possibly a "stringer" up in Gilpin County, writing on local affairs for the Denver paper—never spoke to Aunt Clara, but was simply reporting the gossip on the street. The arrival of 16 (or 26, or 34) southern blacks in a small community like Central City would have been cause for a great deal of public comment and speculation, and it's likely that the details would have been supplied by storytellers who didn't really have the facts.[15]

Thomson, on the other hand, was carrying on a pleasant conversation with Clara, who no doubt rambled over the course of their six-hour stagecoach ride together. It is not hard to imagine that, at times, Clara would have referred to the emigrants as her "children," and Thomson was probably already confused by the references to her as "Aunt." But in recounting their plight, she would have no doubt mentioned that some were orphaned.

Burrell's account, probably based on personal acquaintance but not on a direct interview, simply used the convenient "relatives," while the *Republican* interviewer probably got closer to the facts of the matter. At any rate, given what little we know of the emigrants, it seems they weren't close relatives.

Bruyn identified one of the settlers as Jack (Jackson) Smith. The Jackson Smith reference gets a little confusing, as there was another black man with that name who was in Colorado even before Clara, working as a pressman for William Byers' *Rocky Mountain News*.[16] But Smith was living in the same residence as Clara according to the 1870 census, and his connection to her later in life supports that he could have been one of those she brought back from the east.[17]

Years later, banker Frank Young wrote about Clara and her circle in his privately published memoir, *Echoes From Arcadia*:

> *Everyone knew and recognized everyone else, whatever might be the positive difference of social position. In this connection I might speak of Aunt Clara Brown. She was raised in old Kentucky, and with her own freedom secured after years of persistent, patient toil, when well along in life she joined the procession of gold seekers to Gregory gulch. Through the unusual returns of a mining camp for labor such as hers, she was able to bring out from the old plantation her children and later her children's children; and with them, whether aided by her efforts or stimulated by her example, have, year after year, come many others of her race, worthily represented by the Poynters, the Lees, the Nelsons and other families who are as tenacious of recognition as you or I might be.*[18]

The Lees we have already met. The Nelsons, William and Susan, were a prominent black family in Central City—the 1870 census gives his real estate holdings a value of $1500. They were certainly friends of Clara's; William Nelson actually signed for some county warrants paid to Clara in 1874. But he was from Massachusetts and she from South Carolina, so they were certainly not among those Clara brought back from Kentucky and Tennessee.

Henry Poynter is another well-known figure in Central City, but the official information about him is confusing. There is a Henry *Pointer* listed in the 1860 census; it says he was a cook, aged 36, and born in Kentucky. But in the 1870 census his age is given as 42, and in the 1880 census he's listed as 58, so his exact age is difficult to determine. He was married—both he and his wife, Juda (or Judah) are listed on a complicated land transaction in the Clear Creek County records involving Aunt Clara.[19]

Poynter stayed in Central City until his death and became a respected member of the community. Caroline Bancroft, in her dramatization of Central City pioneer history, *Gulch of Gold,* was probably relying on the reminiscences of Young in recounting the following story of the great Central City fire of 1874:

58

> As Frank excitedly realized that the fire would
> soon reach the First National Bank at the corner of Main
> and Eureka Streets, he ran back to the building. Inside, he
> yelled for the janitor, a faithful old darky named Henry
> Poynter (one of the twenty relatives or orphans that Aunt
> Clara Brown had brought to the gulch at the cost of some
> $4,000 of her earnings). Henry Poynter lived in a house on
> Second High Street which Frank presumed the fire would
> not climb to. They found a large lard can and stuffed it full
> of $100,000 in currency and some $300,000 in securi-
> ties.... Then Frank sent the old Negro off through the mael-
> strom in the street to his home....
>
> It was several days before the smoke-blackened
> vault of the First National cooled sufficiently to be touched.
> But when Frank finally opened the doors, he was delighted
> to find that, although some of the papers had been badly
> scorched by the intense heat, every record was legible.
> Eventually faithful Henry Poynter turned up with the lard
> can, saying that he had buried it under his porch. Not a
> dollar was missing.[20]

The Poynters would become very important to Clara in years to come. But the census records clearly demonstrate, and the records of the Gilpin County Pioneer Association confirm, that they had been here long before Clara's rescue mission, so Bancroft's parenthetical remark is obviously in error.

At times, these folks were all involved in business dealings together. In July, 1865, for example, Emily Lee (Jeremiah's wife), William Nelson, Charles and Henry Poynter, and Aunt Clara were all parties in the purchase of some claims on the Gloriana lode from Lorenzo Bowman for $100,[21] a transaction that further demonstrates they were all in Central City before Clara's rescue mission to Kentucky and Tennessee.

Studying the 1870 census records for Central City reveals other pioneer black families who might well have been among those Clara brought back from the east. Taldon (more likely "Talton") Mason, a twenty-six year old laborer, his wife Harriet and six-year-old daughter Susan are all listed as being Kentucky-born, for example. In fact, the Masons were living with Aunt Clara at the time of the census. It seems, moreover, that Clara helped the family find a home-stead; in 1871, she and Talton Mason delivered a quit claim deed for $100 to 160 acres in New York Gulch that contained a log house and stable.

Another family likely to have returned with Clara were the Goodalls. Father Austin (according to the 1870 census) was 45, and Kentucky-born. His wife is not noted—she had perhaps died, or the family was separated during slavery. It was to an "Anthony" Goodall that Clara sold her Mountain City cabin in 1868, for $500; this was probably the same man, and father Goodall was liv-ing in the cabin in 1870 with a number of children—Melvina, Henry, Harriet,

Ella and Aggie, all listed as Tennessee-born.

Two older Goodall daughters had already been married by this time. Sarah wed George Ruby, a teamster from Missouri, in April, 1868,[22] and Margaret married William Mitchell in July. Jackson Smith and Black Hawk's pioneer black barber, Frederick R. Walden, were witnesses at both weddings. Walden had actually purchased a lot and building on Eureka Street from Aunt Clara that same year for $500,[23] and the Goodall's son, 18 years old by the 1870 census, was at that time living with him, and learning the barbering trade. Up Gregory Gulch in the other direction, in Nevadaville, lived Benjamin Brown, a 24-year-old teamster from Missouri, and his 18-year-old wife from Kentucky, Mary; could she, five years earlier, have been one of the orphans Clara supposedly brought back with her?

At any rate, the black emigrants brought back from Kentucky and Tennessee by Aunt Clara seem to have stayed in the Central City and Georgetown areas, where they became useful and productive members of society. At the time of her death, the *Georgetown Courier* noted that she left nine "relatives" in Georgetown,[24] while the *Rocky Mountain Herald* reported that "quite a number now reside" in both the towns.[25]

At that same time, the *Republican* wrote that the original settlers "have long since married and intermarried until they and their descendants form a notable part of the colored community in Colorado."[26] The great Colorado historian LeRoy Hafen, writing years later in *Colorado and Its People*, similarly recognized the growth of Clara's clan, declaring that there "never was a wedding, a large entertainment, or celebration in which some of Aunt Clara's kith and kin did not have a hand."[27]

While they received, over the years, an increasing amount of acceptance from the white community, the black residents always took care of their own. They were involved in business dealings together, and socialized together, the *Register* commenting in 1868 that the "colored people of this city had a dance last night, which passed off quietly and respectably and which was doubtless a very pleasant affair. It was well attended."[28]

There is another group of young men and women important to Clara who weren't residents of the area, however. A register of money orders purchased at the Central City post office around this time has survived, and shows that Clara and Jackson Smith sent a number of money orders to some young people at Oberlin, Ohio. In April, 1871, Clara sent funds by this means to Margaret Hall, Nancy and Josephine Smith, and Indiana Bell, and a week later sent another money order to "Maggie" Hall. In May, Jack Smith sent funds to "Nannie" and Josephine Smith, and Maggie Hall. In August, he mailed money to "Nancy Jane" and Josephine Smith, and Margaret Hall, and again in December to Josephine Smith. That following March, Clara again had a money order mailed to Oberlin, this time to Josephine Smith.

Years later, Frank Hall noted in his sketch of Clara, that after bringing her "relatives and children" to Colorado, with the money "still remaining she educated her daughters."[29] While the young women were certainly not her daughters—and may not have been related to her at all— they could well have been somehow related to Jackson Smith. And more than likely, they were among those she had rescued from Kentucky and Tennessee. Oberlin was a logical choice for their education. Both the college there and the community were highly integrated, and both the college and preparatory school were co-educational. Central in developing this progressive attitude were philanthropists Albert and Lewis Tappan, distant relatives of the Lewis Northey Tappan whom Clara knew in Denver.[30] And, of course, her friend and newspaper publisher David C. Collier was an Oberlin graduate.

Records show that there was a Nancy Indiana Bell who was one of Oberlin's first black female students; the other women may only have attended the preparatory school. Whether they returned to Colorado or not is unknown; regardless, they were part of Aunt Clara's growing list of beneficiaries.

The mission to Kentucky and Tennessee, however, along with Clara's ongoing support of the immigrants, began to tell on her own financial status. She appears in assessment rolls for Gilpin County as far back as 1863, when her local holdings were valued at just $500. By 1866, that figure was up to $1200; 1867, $1260 for her properties, plus another $40 for two cows. In 1868, the properties were valued at $1300, and she was assessed another $90 for the cattle and another $60 for five pigs.

Her greatest assessment for her Gilpin properties was in 1869, when she was taxed on $2500; the following year, the figure had slipped to $2000. Her taxes reflected her financial straits; she was delinquent in paying her taxes from 1869 through 1871, not paying until March of 1874. And the levies themselves demonstrate that either she had been liquidating assets, or that they were losing value because of neglect.

In 1868, for example, her taxes—to support county and territorial government, the local schools and road construction—were over $25. By comparison, Henry Poynter paid just over $3 the same year (including a 50¢ poll tax that Clara, as a woman, wouldn't have had to pay). But her taxes for 1869 were down to $19; for 1870, $14.43; and for 1871, just $12.90. By 1872 her property was assessed at just $1500; by the time she came current again, paying her 1873 taxes, her bill was just $9.37.

Certainly, though, Aunt Clara would never have begrudged the new expenses. The closeness, the successes and daily victories of her settlers, friends and (perhaps) relatives must have provided great comfort to Clara. Though she had failed in finding her missing daughter, it is not hard to believe that this growing company of black residents in the mining towns (and across the country!) would have regarded their "Aunt" Clara as head of a diverse, yet united, extended clan. In 1870, the clan paid her the ultimate compliment in that mining community; a location certificate for the "Aunt Clara" claim was filed in Gilpin County for a lode west of High Street in Central City. There were six named discoverers, including Clara herself, Talton Mason, Anthony Goodall, and Jack Nelson Smith.

At least in some sense, she had found a family at last.

Chapter 9

Fortunately, Clara's new "family" had arrived in the mountains at a time when mining activity was on the rebound in Gilpin County and Colorado generally. And better still, one of the clan's elder members had made a major find that would provide wealth and employment for dozens of miners, black and white alike.

The primitive smelting efforts of Lorenzo Bowman, along with those of Caleb Stowell, James Lyon and others, did little to address the growing problem of separating the deep, quartz-based ores from their precious gold, but they were clearly a step in the right direction.

Professor Nathaniel P. Hill, unlike "Professor" Lorenzo Bowman, was a trained metallurgist, rising through the ranks of the faculty at Brown University in Providence, Rhode Island, to that of a full professor. Dispatched by some eastern capitalists to investigate the investment opportunities in Colorado, Hill early fell in with the territorial governor, William Gilpin, and traveled with him to the San Luis valley in southern Colorado to examine Gilpin's land grant there.

Unimpressed with the governor's holdings,[1] Hill naturally gravitated to the center of the state's mining activity, Gilpin County. Recognizing that the area would prove to be his source of livelihood for years to come, Hill purchased a home and lot in Black Hawk for $1800.[2] To quote Burrell's short summary of the professor's career, "his attention was drawn to the imperfect methods of treating the ores of that region, and he devoted much study to the subject.... The better to acquaint himself with his subject, he visited the extensive reduction works at Swansea, in Wales, having first resigned his professorship in Brown University. He spent the winter of 1865-66 in studying ore reduction in Europe, and, in the summer of 1866, made a second voyage to Europe, taking with him seventy tons of Colorado ore for experimental treatment at Swansea."[3]

Gaining positive results from his initial experiments, Hill and his financial backers organized the Boston & Colorado Smelting Company in the spring of 1867. Returning to Colorado, Hill supervised the erection of a mammoth smelting complex along lower Clear Creek at the east end of Black Hawk. Capitalization of the project was for $250,000. One historian recalled that "... the plant at its maximum contained eight groups of buildings, and included seventeen furnaces. It occupied four acres of ground...."[4]

The works only operated for ten years in Black Hawk, from 1868 to 1878; at that time they were relocated to the Denver area to take better advantage of the transportation system that brought ore to the smelters from the fields around the entire state. And Hill's contributions can be overstated, just as those of his own metallurgist, Cornwall-born Richard Pearce, can be underestimated.[5] But certainly Hill's contribution was real, and well recognized; he was elected to the U.S. Senate from Colorado in 1879.[6] Gold production in Gilpin County rose from just under $1 million in 1867 to $1.6 million in 1868, and to nearly $2.7 million in 1869.

At the same time as Hill's smelter led the way to profitable recovery of additional gold from the ores, new mining techniques, organization and financing were enabling mines to produce wealth in quantities unrealized since the bonanza days of John Gregory in 1859. Take, for example, the legendary Bobtail mine in Black Hawk. Though sullied by the rampant speculation of the Civil War years, the mine was fortunate in that its eastern owners persevered, and in 1864 sent out a qualified Pennsylvania engineer, Andrew N. Rogers, to supervise the operations.

Rogers worked to consolidate the various holdings along the Bobtail vein. He started the system of tunnels that eventually grew to over thirty miles, and bought, built, or expanded stamp mills until the company had 125 stamps for ore processing. "It could boast of a gold production in the decade after '64 of three and a half million dollars. A hundred tons of ore were produced each day, the production value of which amounted to some $5,000 per month. It provided employment for 500 men...."[7]

With the smelters, mills and mines in full operation through the late 1860's and early 1870's, jobs for Clara's settlers should have been plentiful. Whether black miners would have been welcomed, however, is another question. Though labor was scarce, discrimination was nonetheless common.

One area in which that discrimination was obvious was in Central City's fledgling public school system. Schools in Central had been operated since at least 1862; when the city was chartered on March 11, 1864, the incorporation act gave the city the right to establish "a school for the education of white children (of said city) over the age of 5 years and under the age of 21 years, for at least 6 months each year, and said school shall be free to all white children within said city; provided, that all taxes raised upon the property (and collected from persons of color) within the City of Central under this act, shall be by the city council set apart and be used exclusively for the education of children of color between the ages of 5 and 21 years, in such manner and under such restrictions as the City Council shall by ordinance provide."[8]

Even with the settlers brought back by Clara, blacks were but a small minority in the county at this time—there were just 4 recorded in the 1860 census, a number that grew to 54 by the 1870 enumeration—and this obviously proved a huge obstacle to the establishment of a school for "children of color." But lest there be any confusion, the city council clarified the barrier still further in its own ordinance that actually created the public school system in the city:

That nothing in the foregoing section shall authorize any child of African descent to attend school with white children: and it shall be lawful for any inhabitants of this city having a child attending said school to make a complaint to the director of said school, or any one of them, requesting them to forbid and prohibit said colored child or children from attending said school; and it shall be the duty of said directors, or any one of them, upon such complaint being made, to forthwith take from said school said colored child or children, and upon the neglect or refusal so to do shall be deemed a neglect of duty in office and misdemeanor, and, on conviction shall be fined a sum not exceeding one hundred dollars; and every request made as aforesaid shall be deemed a separate offense.[9]*

The issue—wonderfully chronicled by University of Colorado associate professor of black studies William M. King—would be a divisive one in Central, one that was a major factor in the bizarre spectacle in 1867 where, "for several months Central had two distinct city governments, one run by the Democrats and one run by the Republicans."[10]

The views reflected in the editorial pages of the *Register*—by this time edited by Clara's old church colleague, David C. Collier, who also served as the superintendent of the county's school district through 1867, and was named chairman of the Central City school board in 1868—and the letters to the editor, demonstrated the city's ambivalence about the rights of its black citizens.

Nor were these overt acts of discrimination simply political ones, with otherwise courteous and fair treatment accorded to the area's African-American residents. Indeed, Clara herself was apparently hectored to a point beyond her considerable tolerance. She complained to Collier, who wrote about the incident in his newspaper:

We are in receipt of a communication from old Aunt Clara, than whom there is not a more respectable, upright colored woman in the territory, in which she complains of some very indecent, disgraceful and insulting language addressed to her on one of our streets by some low-lived fellow who considers himself far her superior. We have only to say that it is never honorable for a big boy to pick on a little boy, or one who claims to be the superior to insult his inferior. No gentleman will do it. Whenever we hear of an attempt on the part of rowdies to maliciously injure any one, whether black or white, no matter how low down the scale of society, we put down the rowdies as lower than those they attempt to injure. In the days of slavery in the south he who would so injure a slave was sure at once to be made to feel the penalties of the law. We mention these things because we have heard of several like instances of late, and they are certainly disgraceful to any community.[11]

Clara's friend Henry Poynter was faced with similar harassment, though he handled it in a very different fashion:

> *An irrepressible conflict occurred yesterday between Henry Poynter, an industrious, honest, worthy and highly respected colored man, and George Donnelly, a white man and something of a bruiser employed in the Eureka foundry. The latter was somewhat intoxicated and began to impose on Poynter, who was passing along the street with a straw mattress. Poynter finally concluded he had borne it long enough, and laid down the mattress and gave Donnelly a severe thrashing, leaving him with a bruised and bloody face in the hands of the police. Poynter was justified by everyone who saw the affray.*[12]

At the same time, the territory was wrestling with the question of granting the vote—the franchise—to its African-American citizens. The right of black males (there was at the time no question of allowing women of any race) to vote had been denied by the failed "Jefferson Territory" organization in 1861, and again in the Colorado Territory's organic act, which granted voting rights only to those "free, white, male, U.S. citizens of twenty-one years, who had been residents of the area on the date of the act's passage." The question would become tied in with the movement for statehood, with Denver's black citizens—Barney Ford[13] prominent among them—playing a major role in delaying efforts to grant Colorado statehood until the objectionable provision was removed.

Even prior to statehood, however, black men were allowed to vote in local elections, and Clara's friends were quick to take advantage. Both Jeremiah Lee and Henry Poynter were listed as voters in the first ward in Central City for the election of 1868. And Poynter's name was listed in the newspaper on a petition urging William Roworth to run for mayor of the town.[14]

Women, of course, couldn't vote, but they could participate in the political process in other ways. Years later, the Poynters signed up as members of the Prohibition party in Gilpin County. And in 1893, both were listed as members of the Equal Suffrage League. Henry Poynter was paid for his service as a witness in a coroner's inquest in 1871, and as a member of the grand jury in the May term in 1873.[15] He was again paid $10 for his service as a grand juror in October, 1877, and $15 as a petit juror the following year.[16]

Still, it's clear that socially, educationally, in the judicial process, even in investing, Clara and her fellow African-American residents faced obstacles not encountered by the white businesspeople of the day. Thomson recounted a litany of Clara's complaints he heard when on their stagecoach ride in 1872:

> *Been much cheated. Has many mining claims taken in payment of debts. Fellow who gave her bill "three months after death." Judge in Denver who let them "jump" her lots, "guess'd such a number had got theirs back couldn't give any more," and man at Blackhawk who jumped her lot and wouldn't even pay for log building on it.*[17]

Despite her experiences Clara continued to use the courts as necessary; there is a reference in the *Register* in June 1870, to "an extensive land case before Judge Kennedy yesterday, relative to the ownership of Aunt Clara Brown and others."[18] In one of her land transactions, in which she gave a quit claim deed to Samuel Quaintance of Black Hawk for some lots along Clear Creek, there is the notation that the property "was recently in controversy in a suit wherein Clara Brown was plaintiff and William M. Crawford & J.J. Crawford the defendants in the District Court...."[19] But there can be little doubt that, the letter of the law notwithstanding, the legal system was stacked against the members of the black community. One such example was documented in the *Register* in 1868:

> *A singular case occurred in the police court yesterday. Some low white man whose name we do not recall, on Thursday met a negro man who is working for Mr. Sabin, on the Casey road. The negro was carrying two pails of water. The white man asked him for a drink. The negro having only the pails refused, when the white man assaulted him and spilled the water. The negro then threw a stone and hit the white man on the head. The latter complained in the police court of the negro who, to avoid difficulty, plead guilty, and was fined five dollars. The City Marshal informs us that the white man was the only really guilty one.[20]*

In other cases, though, the legal system's bias against black citizens was more deadly. A murder case involving two black men dominated the newspapers in 1868. A man named William Hamblin was robbed and murdered in Quartz Valley, northwest of Central City. Deputy Sheriff Brown and Marshal Clark, of Black Hawk, arrested two black men, George Smith and Bob Reynolds. Reynolds escaped, but Smith supposedly "confessed to the murder, and tells how it was done.... It is one of the most brutal murders reported in a long time."[21] Despite such inflammatory coverage, the *Register* simultaneously urged locals to let the legal system run its predictable course: "Many threats of lynching were uttered on the streets. Full justice will doubtless be done to them by the courts, and it is to be hoped that no violence will be done."[22]

Reynolds and Smith had lived near Guy Hill, at the other end of the mining district, east of Black Hawk. Armed with such knowledge, pursuers located Reynolds, but he engaged in a gun battle with them and remained at large.

> *Hearing the facts, Sheriff Grimes secured the services of Wm. Z. Cozens, who went down for him, and will doubtless bring him back dead or alive. Billy Cozens never fails in such cases, and will not on this occasion. Bob is a brutal character and has evidently determined not to be taken alive.[23]*

Reynolds was finally wounded and arrested by Central City's famous lawman, and not surprisingly blamed Smith for the killing of Hamblin. The case became still more complicated when "Edward Fuller, a white boy, was arrested for supposed complicity in the murder of Hamblin.... The testimony was of such a character that Fuller was discharged, as he ought to be."[24]

For some reason, though, the full brunt of the punishment fell upon Smith. The trial concluded in May, when the jury "returned after a short absence with a verdict of guilty. There is no doubt that he will be hanged at an early day."[25] There must have been some cause for concern, however, as the execution, originally scheduled for August, was stayed first once, then again, until February 18, 1870, as the case was appealed to the state's Supreme Court.

The appeal failed, however, and Smith was hanged from a scaffold on Casto Hill, just above Central City. The spectacle offended the reporter for the *Register*, who also commented on the questionable justice of the proceedings:

> *An execution is always revolting to the better feelings of our nature, even though performed within an enclosure which excludes the public gaze. This was doubly so, because it was public and because a crowd, among whom were a few females, attended. The levity exhibited by some of the onlookers showed how low humanity may become debased.... The case of the criminal who expiated his crimes yesterday has been compared a thousand times with that of one who killed a negro a year before, and they say had the murderer been a white man, he never would have been hung. We do not give credence to such a statement, but we do say that these assertions are a proof that the people have lost confidence in the law through the laxity with which it is administered.*[26]

The case of which the reporter speaks is not known. It may have been the well-documented shooting of a black man named Jones, in Georgetown, by a rough named Joe Bush the previous July. After his arrest, Bush boasted that he used to shoot black men "down South, just for the fun of seeing 'em kick."[27]

Closer to home, another case of a white man shooting a black man with little consequence showed that, even a decade later, the system was still stacked against African-Americans. In January, 1878, the *Register* reported that, "[j]ust as we go to press, we learned that Jack Labaree shot and killed the colored man Davidson, with whom he has been quarreling for sometime over a month."[28]

A Coroner's jury found Pearley (Jack) Labaree "feloniously shot and killed said Thomas A. Davidson, intentionally and with malice aforesaid." The *Register* concluded that, "[a]lthough Davidson was very much disliked by the community generally, we do not think that Mr. Labaree had any right to take the law into his own hands as he admits himself he did by arming himself and rushing back to renew the quarrel with Davidson... if Labaree comes off with a final verdict lighter than 'murder' he can consider himself lucky."[29]

The case attracted considerable attention, and two of the area's legal heavyweights: Harper M. Orahood handled the prosecution, while Central City attorney Alvin Marsh, later to be named state attorney general, took the defense:

> *The defendant's counsel, Hon. Alvin Marsh, made the*
> *best of a bad case. He stated that the negro, driving Labaree*
> *away from the stumps in the morning, was dispossessing the*
> *prisoner of his own property, and that he had the right to go*
> *back to work in the afternoon and carry as many firearms as*
> *he chose to defend himself, and that when going down the*
> *highway, being attacked by the negro, was a sufficient ground*
> *for the killing in self-defense.*[30]

The preliminary argument failed to sway Judge Arnold, and Labaree was bound over for trial. The incarceration was somewhat of a joke, however; a few days later Labaree escaped from jail, "easily done with the tools he had secured from some unknown source,"[31] leaving a note promising to return for trial. (He was, however, recaptured two days later and compelled to complete his stay).

The trial itself never came about, the paper reporting that the "indications are that it will hardly be possible to obtain a jury in Gilpin county, as nearly every one called so far has been challenged for cause."[32] The case seems to have made a celebrity of Labaree; within a month he was serving as a local constable, while the *Register* declared that he "may be the next sheriff of Gilpin county...."[33]

Given their second-class legal status, and the demonstrated instances (and half-hearted condemnations) of personal bigotry recounted by Collier in the *Register*, it is likely that the black workingmen introduced by Clara into the economy of the mining camps would have faced considerable resistance. Even if facing outright hostility in the workplace, however, the settlers brought back by Clara were fortunate in having another option. By this time, the varied operations of Jeremiah Lee and Lorenzo Bowman were starting to become major producers—and employers. In addition to their Red, White and Blue Smelting Company, the pair had organized the "Red, White and Blue Mining Company, an organization of colored men operating near Georgetown in 1867."[34]

About this time Lee made several strikes in Clear Creek County, specifically in the "Argentine...a well-known and profitable lode which was discovered at the time of the first silver excitement in the county." Burrell continued that the "O. K. Lode forms part of the nucleus of the group under consideration.... The ore is usually of a good grade, carrying 'sulphurets' and gray copper, and averaging several hundred ounces of silver per ton. The eastern half of the mine is owned by Charles R. Fish and Jeremiah Lee, and up to date this portion has produced not less than $100,000."[35]

This was not just an investment for Lee, however, and the company he and Bowman formed was actively working the lode over the next few years. The mining correspondent for the *Georgetown Miner* wrote in 1869 that "[t]he Red, White and Blue company are working the Argentine lode, on Leavenworth mountain. We were there yesterday and found the shaft 35 feet deep, the crevice being 7 1/2 feet wide, between solid walls. The vein is vertical, trend north-east and south-west. The ore vein is 20 to 24 inches wide, gangue and mineral combined. With proper crushing and concentrating work, this mine can be worked with good profit. We have not seen a better vein in the Territory."[36]

Lee's co-owner in the Argentine, Charles Fish, was also an old friend of Clara's, one of the original ten members that Burrell listed as organizing the congregation that would eventually found St. James Methodist Church in Central City.[37] He lived in Central, a widower with a young son, until 1867, when he moved to Georgetown.[38] He became a notary—he attested to several of the transactions involving Clara, Lee and Bowman and other black mining speculators—and justice of the peace before founding the Bank of Clear Creek at Georgetown.

In fact, through their various property transactions, it is apparent that Clara, and Lee and Bowman, Henry Poynter and other members of the black community were involved in business dealings with, and certainly knew, many of the most prominent business people in the region.

In January 1869, for example, Bowman brought some property from William A. Hamill, a wealthy mine owner who served as state senator from Georgetown and eventually state Republican party chairman.[39] In February, Bowman purchased an interest in a claim from Edward Parmelee, a former city clerk and assessor in Central who became postmaster in Georgetown. Parmelee was also known at the state capitol, serving as clerk of the Senate before being elected state senator himself. And in a complicated transaction involving 23 different claims, Clara and the Poynters were parties, along with Peter McFarlane.

McFarlane, along with his brother Will, owned a foundry and machinery shop in Central City that made equipment for mines and mills all over Colorado and the West. Clara also sold Peter McFarlane a lot she owned on Eureka Street in 1872; the house he built there was his home for nearly 50 years. Besides being a prominent businessman and politician, McFarlane built and—for years after the initial euphoria had worn off—operated the Central City Opera House.[40]

But the Opera House, built in 1878, was probably of little attraction to an aging Aunt Clara. It is much easier to imagine her joy upon the dedication, on Oct. 13, 1873, of a small frame building that was the first permanent home of the First Presbyterian Church of Central City, of which she was apparently a member. The long wooden structure was overshadowed (literally) by the construction the previous year of the stately Teller House hotel on the next lot to the east; a few years later, another large building, the new Opera House, was erected on the lot just to the west.[41]

Every bit as important to Clara—and much more visible—was the completion in 1872, of St. James Methodist Church. As seen above, the Methodist congregation had constructed a church in Central, which opened on Christmas Day, 1860, but burned a year later. After that time, the congregation met in public buildings, first Lawrence Hall, then the county's office and court building, Washington Hall.

The cornerstone for the new building was laid on Eureka Street on

September 10, 1864. Originally the new church was to have been called St. Paul's, but the name was changed to St. James when the Episcopal church in town adopted the former title.[42]

Certainly Clara's contributions to the new Methodist church—besides providing space for services prior to the construction of the first building—were significant. One later newspaper account even provided that "the white protestants desired to build a church, but could not raise the necessary means, and Aunt Clara, as she was generally called, came forward, and out of her own hard-earned money donated almost enough to build the donated edifice; the only colored person among the many that were there, she gave more than all the whites; and thus, through her instrumentality, was built the first Protestant church in the Rocky mountains."[43]

This is no doubt overstated, since the building ultimately cost $42,000,[44] but there's no doubt that Clara stayed in supportive contact with the congregation even after her uniting with the Presbyterian Church in Central City. But an even greater source of financial support probably came from the increasing numbers of Cornish miners, most of whom were Methodists, who began arriving in the gulch communities in the late 1860's.

So the funds available for construction grew in the 1860's, and the congregation began building the lower level of the edifice. Bad luck dogged the project again, as in the summer of 1868 it was discovered that the basement walls were poorly constructed and would have to be rebuilt.[45] Finally, McFarlane's firm, Barclay & Company, was awarded the contract, and work progressed smoothly. The church's inspiring stained glass windows were installed in 1871, and the structure was completed and dedicated, by Bishop R.S. Foster, on July 21, 1872.

McFarlane also benefited from the work involved in rebuilding Central City after its great fire of May 21, 1874. It was not the first fire in the town's history, and Clara herself had been involved in at least two others. The first was in April, 1872:

> *Last evening, about five o'clock, the citizens living in the vicinity of McCall and Lewis' Central Barn, were startled by the cry of fire. Messrs. Giddings, Lewis, and Sabin, were in the aforesaid barn at the time, engaged in conversation, when the alarm was given. Hastily picking up buckets and filling them with water, they rushed to the scene, and found that the house on fire belonged to Aunt Clara Brown. Through their united efforts the fire was extinguished. It is supposed to have originated from a defective flue.[46]*

Byers' *Rocky Mountain News*, assuming that its Denver readers would know Aunt Clara, wrote that "[a]n imperfect flue is what set Clara Brown's house at Central on fire the other night."[47]

Whether that was Clara's home and business location on Lawrence Street is not made clear, but she almost certainly lost that property in a major fire the following year. That January sixteen buildings on lower Lawrence Street—below the brick building known as Raynold's Court—were destroyed in a fire that caused $20,000 in property losses. The fire started in the flue of the old Episcopal Church, St. Paul's; that wooden building was later rebuilt as a $10,000 stone edifice on First High Street.[48]

Fire fighting efforts largely consisted of tearing down some of the more ramshackle buildings to prevent the blaze from spreading. "This however failed and three small buildings, belonging to Aunt Clara Brown (colored), were soon wrapped in the flames."[49] Sadly, Clara seems to have had no insurance on the buildings. She had apparently bought the properties in October, 1868, with a $1,000 deed of trust to James Kidd. With renters in the buildings, she was no doubt able to cover the payments, even at the outlandish interest rate of 2 1/2 percent a month! But once the homes were destroyed, she had no income to pay the note; by the following October, the total debt was up to $2,370, and Kidd reclaimed the lots at a Trustee's Sale October 15th.[50] Clara certainly had other properties—the 1869 tax rolls, for example, listed not only three houses on Lawrence Street, but two on High Street, with a total assessed valuation of $2,500. (Compare this to Henry Poynter's modest home on 3rd High Street, assessed at just $150). But there's no doubt this loss greatly impacted her future earnings.

Even that 1873 conflagration was but a prelude to the great 1874 fire. Various accounts of the fire's origins exist—many put the source in a "Chinese laundry in Dostal Alley,"[51] and invented tales to explain the outbreak—but of the outcome there can be no question. One hundred and fifty buildings were destroyed, at a cost of approximately $230,000.

The fire—and the succeeding building boom—transformed Central City. One observer wrote that "[b]y the end of 1874 scores of new brick and stone buildings graced the main streets of the town. Leveled and graded streets, sidewalks, and here and there handsome store fronts of ironwork provided a touch of elegance missing in the old clapboard and log cabin town perched precariously on both sides of the gulch."[52]

But another construction project would have thrilled Aunt Clara even more. By the 1870's Jeremiah Lee had prospered in many ways. Not only had his Clear Creek County investments made him a wealthy man, but his wife Emily had presented him with a fine family; daughters Alice and Sarah, now teenagers, had been born in Missouri, while two younger children, John and Catherine (Kate), had arrived after the Lees' relocation to Colorado in 1863.

To provide for his growing family in the style that his wealth made possible for him, Lee decided to build a grand house in Central City. Purchasing land from local businessman and Central City mayor Jacob Kruse (Ida Kruse McFarlane of Opera House fame was his niece), the Lees began building a house out of the local "Hooper" brick used in so much of the post-fire business construction, but rarely for private homes. The square two-story home was the finest on West High Street, which became known as "Banker's Row" because of the number of wealthy financiers living there.

Lee, however, was not among them. Instead, the brick mansion was rented out to banker Thomas Hale Potter, while the more numerous Lee family lived in a small frame cabin in the rear of the lot. In her notes for her 1970 biography of Aunt Clara, author Kathleen Bruyn can be seen wrestling with this anomaly, trying to find a "reason" why bankers were not allowed to live in their own houses.[53]

There was no reason, of course; the presence of a number of bankers along the very street demonstrates the nonsense of such thinking. And so Bruyn's book, along with a number of later newspaper articles,[54] just ignored the question entirely. A sadder explanation comes to mind; that Lee, despite his wealth and prominence, was still thought of first and foremost in Central City as a black man, and thus unworthy to live in the finest house in town.[55] One wonders if overt threats were made, or just subtle hints, that led Jeremiah Lee to conclude that, for his family's safety, it would be best to display his wealth in less ostentatious fashion.

The whole curious incident is in some ways a microcosm of the African-American experience in 1870's Central City. With the passage of the federal civil rights act in 1866, the 13th, 14th and 15th amendments to the U.S. Constitution, and the statehood of Colorado in 1876, blacks had more legal protections than ever before. In Central City, Clear Creek County, and throughout Colorado, they used these new freedoms to buy property, start businesses, and in many cases become wealthy and respected members of society.

But their social status was still, somehow, suspect. Even their white defenders were, even if inadvertently, condescending, while outright opposition occasionally revealed itself in print and in person. Even Aunt Clara, respected though she was, had often been subject to the less admirable and unspoken strictures of the "Little Kingdom of Gilpin."

Still, for Clara, this must have been a satisfying time. The little town in which she had made her home had grown into a handsome city, the fulcrum for political power in the state of Colorado and a center for culture and civility in what had been a wild frontier land. She had seen the religious community she supported develop into an establishment, with large congregations worshipping in a host of splendid churches.

As for her fellow African-Americans, they had achieved a level of wealth and prominence unimagined a decade earlier. The emigrants she brought back from war-torn Kentucky and Tennessee were now a major part of a growing band of black businessmen, mine owners and workingmen and women who must have had deep feelings for their matriarch and benefactress.

For Clara, now in her seventies, this should have been a time of well-earned rest. Despite being the victim of numerous frauds and financial reverses, she would still have had considerable property holdings producing income. Perhaps, some forty years after their separation, she had grown accepting of the fact that she would never locate her missing daughter. She could look back on two decades of good works in Colorado, efforts to help her people that must have succeeded beyond her greatest expectations.

But Clara, ever ready to answer a cry of distress from her black brothers and sisters, was not to have such a period of quiet retirement. Again, a call for help came, from a most unexpected location. And as always, she would answer the call.

Chapter 10

While the free blacks of Colorado had been prospering, the ex-slaves remaining in the South were not faring nearly so well. Clara's circle in Central City was well aware of the hardships that their black brothers and sisters were suffering in the war-ravaged South, and took steps to provide assistance as best they could. The *Register* recognized one such effort in 1867:

> *We again call attention to the Festival and supper to be given by the colored people on Wednesday evening, April 24th. The exercise of charity in opening one's purse as well as in words and thoughts is the noblest characteristic of noble men and women, and we therefore announce this Festival with pleasure. Its design is to raise funds to assist in the relief of their bretheren [sic] freedmen of the South. Already they have received great assistance from the citizens of Central in their enterprise, for which they return thanks. But they need further assistance in this matter. People can not give to a more worthy object. All who desire to attend are cordially invited.*[1]

The following week, the paper reported on the outcome of the festivities: one wonders if David Collier himself was the reporter who attended.

> *We attended the festival given by our colored citizens last evening, in the basement of St. Paul's church. The room was well filled, the colored people from Central and Black Hawk being nearly all present. We have seldom seen a more orderly, or a more pleasant assemblage. We were also glad to note the presence of a number of our best citizens with their families, who were contributing liberally to the cause.... Of the proceeds we cannot state this morning, but whatever they may be, they will be expended under the advice of Rev. Mr. Jennings, who with Rev. Mr. Crawford and Rev. Mr. Fuller, were present during the evening. It is due to say that the whole affair is an effort on the part of our colored citizens to aid their brethren at the South, and their success reflects on them the highest credit.*[2]

For the ex-slaves of the South, the promise of emancipation, of the Freedman's Bureaus, of public education, was never fully realized. As another decade passed, with the end of Reconstruction, the "redeemed" southern states began to impose, through legislation and extra-judicial intimidation, policies that threatened to erode what few gains black citizens there had won.

At the same time that the dreams of the Reconstruction era were fading, in the late 1870's a new hope began to emerge—and that hope was in Kansas.

The movement began in an orderly enough fashion, spurred by Benjamin "Pap" Singleton. Born a slave in 1809 in Nashville, Tennessee, Singleton several times escaped but was recaptured. Eventually succeeding in his flight, he went first to Canada, then moved back across the national boundary to Detroit, where he ran a boardinghouse that frequently housed his fellow run-aways. Returning to Union-controlled Nashville during the Civil War, Singleton, who had been trained as a cabinetmaker, built coffins while living in a camp for fugitive slaves.

By 1869, Nashville had passed back from Republican control to Democratic, and the prospects for the newly freed blacks in the area were growing increasingly grim. Singleton and a black preacher, Columbus Johnson, organized a homestead association. The association sent a committee to investigate conditions in Kansas, thinking that blacks could take advantage of laws that would allow them to homestead on former federal lands there, and as early as 1873 Singleton, Johnson and 300 other black settlers departed by steamboat for Wyandotte and Topeka, Kansas.

Despite fervid white opposition, the movement to emigrate to Kansas picked up steam, with supporters organizing conventions in Nashville, Vicksburg, and Houston. Singleton formed the Edgefield Real Estate and Homestead Association, and between 1874 and 1879 is estimated to have moved 20,000 black migrants from Tennessee.

Others took up the Kansas colonization movement. A white Indiana preacher named W. R. Hill began a colony originally named Hill City in the fall of 1876; as the colony grew with additional arrivals from Kentucky and Missouri in 1877 and 1878, the town's name was changed to Nicodemus.[3]

But the colony struggled, and good-hearted men and women of both races provided financial and other assistance. Word of the colony's need even reached Gilpin County which, no doubt inspired by the hardworking black community there, was quick to send aid of its own. A collection was taken up, the results of which were recorded in a "Card of Thanks" printed by the solicitor, J. W. Niles, in the *Register*:

> *I hereby return my sincere thanks to the citizens of Central and Black Hawk for the timely aid they have rendered me in behalf of the needy Nicodemus Colony of Grand county, Kansas. I have received from Central $26.25 in cash and about $50.00 worth of good warm clothing. From Black Hawk I received $17.50 in cash, all of which will be faithfully applied to the relief of the sufferers, who will greatly appreciate the liberal contributions....*[4]

But thousands of destitute and persecuted blacks from the Deep South heard greatly embellished tales of the opportunities to be found, and dispensing with any organization or sponsorship, tried to somehow make it to the promised land of Kansas. The reasons for the emigration were obvious enough, even to the writers of the Central City *Register*, a thousand miles away. Always a good Republican organ, the paper had railed against Ku Klux Klan "horrors" as early as 1871,[5] and in 1874 reported that the "wholesale slaughter of Negroes is reported from Tennessee, Kentucky, Louisiana and Alabama. The whites charge that the negroes have conspired to drive out or kill the whites in certain localities, and their friends claim that the conspiracy is on the part of the whites, and the object aimed at is to prevent the negroes from holding office or coming to the polls on election day."[6]

This disorganized migration, reflecting the deep religious faith and almost apocalyptic beliefs of the migrants, soon became known as the "Black Exodus," and the migrants themselves as the "Exodusters." But lacking any sort of support system or financial resources, the exodus quickly turned into a disaster of biblical proportions. Whites along the Mississippi took up arms to prevent the transient blacks from camping along the river, waiting for passage. Riverboats refused to pick up migrating blacks, even those with full fare, while "merchants and planters threatened to withdraw their patronage if they carried such cargo."[7] Others—white and black alike—passed themselves off as "conductors," taking the small amounts of money saved by the refugees and promising steamboat and train tickets which, of course, were never delivered.

The result of the chaos along the Mississippi was a large, ever-shifting concentration of homeless, impoverished black families. Yellow fever began to ravage many of the river towns in Mississippi, Louisiana and Missouri, providing further arguments for those settlers—again, white and black—already in Kansas who adamantly opposed the influx. The *Chicago Journal* wrote that a "report is current that the white settlers in Kansas are organizing into bands to prevent any more negroes from entering the State, and that certain companies patrol the river to prevent the steamboats from landing any cargoes of negroes."[8]

Once the emigrants had reached Kansas, they still faced difficult times. The *Wyandotte Gazette*, a black newspaper, reported on a delegation from the southern states that had toured the black settlements in Kansas:

> As regards the prospects of colored emigrants to the State there was considerable diversity of opinion, the majority apparently taking the view that the colored man who possessed some capital, sufficient to stock a small farm, might do well, while those dependent entirely upon daily labor would have a pretty hard row to hoe. A number of the colored members of the party remained in Kansas, but their places were all filled on the return train, one of the managers said, by some of the earlier colored immigrants from the South, who were very glad of the opportunity to get back to their old homes. The Associated Press reporter at St. Louis sums up the various opinions as follow: "The weight of testimony is decidedly against the emigration of poor negroes to Kansas."[9]

The mass immigration was the primary subject of newspaper articles throughout Kansas. Even in Clara's former home, it was reported that "[t]hese unfortunates form the chief topic of conversation in Leavenworth, as elsewhere. They are crowded into churches and vacant buildings all over the city."[10] Throughout eastern Kansas, the emigrants "faced severe problems, largely caused by their sudden arrival in such great numbers. Later Singleton…and other black leaders would advise those leaving the South not to head toward Kansas, so strained were its relief facilities."[11]

But others in Kansas, both white and black, welcomed, or at least recognized the inevitability of the movement, and sought ways to ameliorate the worst of the suffering it created. As early as May, 1879, a "large meeting of the colored citizens of Topeka was held on the evening of Monday for the purpose of forming a permanent organization to look after the interests of the colored emigrants to Kansas, and to render necessary aid to such of the emigrants as really demand it."[12]

The report continued that the new organization, the Kansas Colored State Emigration Bureau, "has already extended aid to many destitute refugees, and as the relief fund in the hands of the officers of the bureau is nearly exhausted, gifts of money would be quite acceptable."[13]

As the summer arrived, and the massive influx continued, conditions became even more dire. Reverend T. W. Henderson, who had served as corresponding secretary of the largely black emigration bureau, was just one of many board members appointed to a new organization, the Kansas Freedman's Relief Association. Their manifesto, published in Topeka on June 26, 1879, was addressed "To the Friends of the Colored People," and read in part:

> The directors of the Kansas Freedman's Relief Association, in view of the present situation, deem it proper to make public this address, and ask the friends of the colored people to further aid in caring for the helpless and destitute refugees.
>
> This is a matter not local to our State, but is one of national concern. It involves the solution of a great question, important alike to people of the whole country, and if properly met will go very far to work a cure of the ills of the freedmen of the South. If we prove equal to the occasion, and can assist these people who are seeking homes in the North, and utilize their labor, those who remain behind will discover a kindlier feeling and better treatment in the South.
>
> In organizing this association, we are moved by two controlling motives. The first was one of humanity. Many of them were old and decrepit, and many young and helpless, and with few exceptions were destitute. They were landed on the river banks by hundreds, in the chilly days of early spring, after a long and tedious journey, fraught with hardships and

privations. Many were sick and dying from exposure, and many were suffering for food, clothing and medical assistance. The simplest dictates of humanity demand immediate and organized effort for their relief.

Another incentive to meet this emergency was to maintain the honored traditions of our State which had its conception and birth in a struggle for freedom and equal rights for the colored man. She has shed too much blood for this cause to now turn back from her soil these defenseless people fleeing from the land of oppression.

We have not sought to stimulate or encourage their migration hither. We have always endeavored to place before the colored people of the South the plain facts, hoping thus to properly restrain an improvident hegira based upon delusive hopes and expectations. We have also sought to impress upon them that other Western and Northern states possess equal advantages for homes for the laboring man. In brief, we have undertaken, so far as lies in our power, to provide for the destitute of these people, who come voluntarily among us, the common necessities of life, and to assist them in obtaining situations where they can earn a livelihood....

This association has taken charge of, and aided more or less, about three thousand of these people, and there are still here and on the way from St. Louis about four hundred more. We have received money from all sources, $5,819.70. We have expended and incurred obligations for the whole of this fund. A large quantity of clothing and blankets have been received, and we have a large lot of clothing now on hand. What we need is money with which to obtain shelter, medical assistance, and furnish transportation to such places as will give them employment. This we must have, or relinquish all further efforts at organized assistance to these refugees.

The good people who have already so generously contributed to the cause, have our sincere thanks.

All contributions should be sent to Gov. John P. St. John.[14]

The Kansas governor served as president of the organization, which also included justices from the state supreme court and U.S. district court, and the Kansas attorney general and secretary of state. With such august patronage, support and funds began arriving from all over the country, and even the world. The organization collected "over a hundred thousand dollars for relief. One-fourth of the aid came from English sympathizers in the form of Staffordshire pottery. Philip D. Armour, after a personal tour of Wyandotte, Kansas, collected twelve hundred dollars in donations from Chicago industrialists, and, together with beef from his meat-packing plant, sent it on to the black refugees."[15]

As early as April of 1879, Governor St. John had received $33 from Central City, "that sum being the proceeds of an entertainment given for the benefit of the refugees."[16] And other aid from Colorado was to follow. By May of 1879, word of the refugees' plight had reached Denver. At that point were "the citizens of Denver called together to adopt measures of relief for the colored emigrants."[17] Probably the one issuing the call was the Reverend Robert Seymour, pastor of the African Methodist Episcopal Church.

Seymour chaired the convocation, and his speech at the meeting was noted with approbation in the Denver *Tribune*. Seymour declared that, as he was summarized in the *Tribune*, "there was a better way of disbursing the money raised than sending it to Kansas; that the donation of a little money would only be a partial and temporary relief and that the aim in view should be broader and more comprehensive. It should include not only assistance for the present but be directed intelligently so as to become a part of a plan for the permanent good of the emigrants. In other words, the committee should endeavor to bring some of the emigrants to Colorado and colonize them here."[18] The remainder of the column, which could at best be characterized as paternalistic, replayed the same theme over and over again. Worse still, as the *Rocky Mountain News* reported, the gathering was "very poorly attended."[19]

The *Tribune* reporter followed up by interviewing a number of local politicians on the prospects for settling some of the Kansas blacks in Colorado. Former territorial governor John Evans replied that "I think that a number of colored men could do well here, but that they ought not to be brought in indiscriminately." Richard Sopris, now mayor of Denver, said that "a moderate immigration of negroes into Colorado would rebound to our advantage as well as to theirs. They could be made useful in hundreds of ways. As house servants the negroes are scarcely excelled anywhere.... They do excellent work in the mines as well as in the fields, and might find plenty of employment on the railroads which are now being built...."[20]

An executive committee was formed, headed by Governor Frederick W. Pitkin, "whose task it was to raise funds for those stranded in Kansas. Former governor John Evans, whose philanthropy was widely known, set the drive in motion with a hundred-dollar contribution. The *News* was pleased to report that representatives from Colorado's small Negro community came to the meeting and showed an interest in the cause."[21]

Pitkin communicated the gist of the Denver plan to his colleague in Kansas, Governor St. John, noting that the "marvelous tide of immigration toward Colorado & our mining camps brings the sick & the destitute. We are called upon to minister to the suffering emigrants in our midst & in spite of our great mineral wealth we expect to have the poor always with us." He continued that "if the refugees in Kansas really were suffering and if that state could not provide enough aid, Colorado would contribute; otherwise he wanted to spend funds that had been raised locally for transportation costs."[22]

Even the *New York Times* picked up on the potential Colorado connection;

within days of the Colorado meetings, it was reporting that the state was welcoming to the emigrants, so "let us help them wisely."[23]

Governor St. John sent a letter to lawyer Wilmer Walton, who was apparently soliciting aid in Denver:

> *Your telegram of the 29th duly received. While we are in need of funds yet, we are more greatly in need of homes for destitute freedmen, and we hope that the good people of Denver may feel inclined to furnish employment for a hundred. This would not only be a great relief to our committee, but would accomplish more from a financial standpoint, than a donation of a thousand dollars in cash.*[24]

And while the impact, if not the intent, of Seymour's speech, and the entire resettlement plan, was probably to decrease cash donations, apparently some were received. Though the *News* characterized Denver's black community as "small," it certainly had its prosperous members, who doubtless opened their pocketbooks in response to Rev. Seymour's appeal. Barney Ford, Clara's onetime lodger in Mountain City, was preeminent among them. "By the 1870's, journalists estimated Ford's aggregate wealth at a quarter of a million dollars."[25]

H. O. Wagoner, Ford's relative and sometimes partner, owned "valuable property on Blake Street, near Nineteenth, and other pieces scattered around in various parts of the City," according to a *Republican* article in 1890, while "William H. Green, the barber on Nineteenth street…is rated at something like $40,000." Another barber-entrepreneur, Ed Sanderlin, "came to Denver and opened the first barber shop and restaurant. He has gradually made and saved money, and now has property scattered around all over the city and in the State." In fact, the article concluded that there were "fully 100 colored men who are worth from $5,000 to $10,000 each, and a few who range from $20,000 to $150,000."[26] This was out of a statewide black population of 6,215 in that year, up dramatically from the 2,435 a decade earlier.

And Clara herself was continuing to buy and sell properties, usually at a handsome profit. In 1874, for example, she sold a home in East Denver to John L. Dailey, Denver's first parks commissioner, for $300. Surely she would have given of her own small fortune to the fundraising effort. But for Clara, typically, that wasn't enough.

University of Colorado historian Robert Athearn wrote an impressive study of the black migration to Kansas, and summarized the next developments as follows:

> *Colorado civic leaders were anxious to learn something of the Kansas situation before committing money to the cause. When "Aunt" Clara Brown, a black woman who was well known in Denver and Central City, offered to investigate the situation, Governor Pitkin agreed at once. He wrote a letter of introduction to St. John, explaining who Aunt Clara was: "She came to Colorado in 1859 & accumulated quite a large fortune,*

*but has spent most of it for the relief of her own race. She is one
of the best old souls that ever lived & is respected and loved by
all who know her. She goes to Kansas to see the destitute freedmen & to report here upon their condition." Help her, said
Pitkin, and give her suggestions "as you think will promote the
object she has in view."*[27]

Her return was noted in the Central City newspaper in September, 1879:

*Aunt Clara Brown, whom everybody in Central knows,
returned from a visit to Kansas some few days since, whith-
er...she went to look into the condition of the colored refugees,
and in the interest of the sufferers generally. There are about
5,000 of them all told, and they are getting on as fast as could be
expected. The greater portion have found employment, and the
balance will, doubtless, in the course of time. Aunt Clara says
they are an industrious and sober class of people, who only ask
an opportunity to make an honest living. Their cry is work, work,
and that is being given them as fast as possible. She was kindly
received by Gov. St. John and the people generally. She thinks
that in another year these people will be well to do and self-sup-
porting.*[28]

Exactly what Clara's activities were in Kansas remains unclear. No
records, either in Kansas or Colorado, detailing her mission have been found.
Perhaps she did go with the intention of bringing refugees back to work in
Colorado, as Governor St. John suggested, and as she earlier did with the ex-
slaves from Kentucky and Tennessee. But as in that post-war period, it is anything but certain that the potential immigrants would have received a warm
reception. As Athearn put it:

*Labor was in great demand among mine owners, and
thousands of Italians, Irish, Austrians, Serbs, Slovenes, Croats,
and other newly arrived immigrants answered the call. Yet, by
1880, labor conditions became so turbulent that in May the
Leadville mines were shut down by strikers, and Governor Pitkin
was obliged to call out the militia in order to protect property.
This was not a good time or a good place for blacks to be introduced as cheap labor, and many of them undoubtedly shunned
the idea as they had when opportunities had been given them to
work in the Missouri coal mines.*[29]

So perhaps Clara went to deliver funds, and to assure that they went to
appropriate uses. There is record of the Kansas Freedman's Relief Association
receiving money from Colorado sources: a "Statement of receipts and expendi-
tures" for the organization in July, 1879, for example, listed the $33 contribution
noted above from Central City, another $50 from "colored people" in Pueblo,
along with individual contributions of $5 each from a John McGee in Pueblo and

82

a W. C. Campbell in Alpine.[30] But if Clara brought money, it was a small amount; by October 13, the Kansas Freedmen's Relief Association reported that the total contributions from Colorado were just $155.70 (compared to nearly $3000 from Ohio, and over $1500 from both Pennsylvania and New York.)[31] If Clara simply went to see the Exodusters to "report on their condition," as Pitkin suggested, her great heart must surely have been touched by the spectacle.

This endeavor is less well known than Clara's earlier return to Kentucky and Tennessee in 1865. Burrell didn't mention it at all in his biographical sketch of her written about the same time,[32] nor did the several lengthy *Denver Republican* articles of the early 1880's. But it in many ways is no less remarkable.

First, it's clear from Governor Pitkin's letter that she was in some sense acting as an official representative for the Colorado relief effort. That an African-American woman in her late seventies would be so designated is surprising, and illustrates the high regard in which Aunt Clara was held statewide by that time. How fantastic it would have seemed to Clara, as a slave child growing up in Virginia and Kentucky, that she would one day be representing the governor of one state as an emissary to another!

Second, her own willingness to undertake such a trip at all at her advanced age speaks volumes about her continued philanthropy. Though she now could travel in relative comfort to Kansas by train, this was still a strenuous pilgrimage by such an elderly woman in that day.

Finally, it is worth noting that Clara undertook such a journey for her black brothers and sisters. Certainly there was need enough among all the races in Denver and Colorado at that time. In fact, an associate of Clara's, Frances Wisebart Jacobs, was initiating programs in the same period that would earn her fame as Denver's "mother of charities." Jacobs came to Central City in 1863 with her husband, pioneer Jewish merchant Abraham Jacobs, whose O. K. Store would certainly have been known to Clara. Abraham Jacobs later opened a store in Denver, where his wife became increasingly active in charity work. She founded the Denver Hebrew Ladies' Relief Society in 1872, but soon "realized that the problems of poverty, sickness, malnutrition, and unsanitary living conditions were not limited to the Jewish community."[33]

Determined to help all the suffering in Denver, she helped organize the Denver Ladies' Relief Society just two years later. In 1887, she joined her efforts to those of the city's Congregational church and Catholic archdiocese to form the Charity Organization Society, an umbrella organization that was the forerunner of the United Way charitable trust.

Clara, too, worked tirelessly to help all those in need. The many accolades she received later in life, as well as the eulogies and honors after her death, were always quick to point out her good works, the *Republican* noting that "she engaged in numerous noble charities; turned her home into a hospital, a hotel, and a general refuge for those who were sick or in poverty. If those who made her house their home were able to pay her for what they received, she accepted it, if not, it did not matter."[34] Considering that all these accounts were written by white males, and that none mentioned her particular service to sufferers of any race, she must have been a truly ecumenical giver.

At times, these charitable efforts were subsidized by the local government: throughout the 1860's and 1870's, for example, county warrants were written to Aunt Clara for "keeping pauper," or "taking care Mrs. Myers." In the latter case, Clara received two warrants in October, 1870, one for $14.85, the other for $43.60. Nor were Clara's ministrations limited to the living; in 1873, she received a warrant for $2 for "laying out body of Mrs. Goldsboro."[35]

But these fine works should not obscure the fact that the defining efforts of her charitable life—her rescue mission to Kentucky and Tennessee in 1865, and this 1879 relief mission to Kansas—were both undertaken on behalf of the indigent and suffering among her fellow African-Americans. Once again, though, there may have been an ulterior motive as well. With thousands of poor southern blacks streaming into Kansas, she may again have hoped to find—or find word of—her missing daughter, Eliza Jane. If so, she was once more disappointed. But she would not remain disappointed for long; goodness was at last to be rewarded.

Chapter 11

Besides being physically challenging, the trip to Kansas must have further taxed Aunt Clara's dwindling finances, as well. Combined with her declining health, this aged woman who had given so much to so many during her years in Colorado now found herself needing to rely on the kindness of others. She moved from Central City, her home for 20 years, to Denver, and found herself living in a "little white frame house that sets [*sic*] back from the street."[1]

Typically, the *Denver Republican* provided the most coverage of Aunt Clara's later years; also typically, the coverage is confusing and sometimes contradictory. The address of the "little white frame house" is given in an 1882 article as 597 Arapahoe Street, in 1884 as 517, and in 1885 as 607.[2] But all the accounts agree that the home was not her own. As one *Republican* article put it: "Misfortune came upon her in sundry ways, and she was reduced to poverty, having to depend upon those who had known her in other circumstances for aid. Mr. Charles Cheever provided a comfortable home for her at 517 Arapahoe street...."[3]

Chever (the usual spelling) was one of the original Colorado pioneers, arriving in Auraria in August 1859. Though born in Salem, Massachusetts, he came to Colorado from Oroville, California, in that state's gold mining country. He was elected Arapahoe County clerk and recorder in 1861 and served eight years. In the decades that followed he became one of downtown Denver's major landowners. His first major building, the Chever block at 17th and Larimer, was constructed in 1879. He followed that with the Arapahoe Building, 1616-22 Arapahoe, and the Essex Building, 1617 Lawrence, in 1888.[4]

He was apparently by nature a charitable fellow, at one point hosting a benefit for the early Colorado thespian Jack Langrishe, when that much-loved actor was down on his luck.[5] He would probably have known Clara during her stay in the Cherry Creek towns, and as clerk and recorder would at least have known of her from her many real estate transactions. So if she were truly indigent by the early 1880's, he could well have known of it, and thought to provide a home for someone he knew and admired.

Still, this seems strange in several respects. First, we recall—as would have Chever—the listings of Clara's real estate holdings in the 1860's, which included "sixteen lots in Denver."[6] But the same article continued that "designing men swindled her in declining years, and to-day she is almost an object of charity. She has a life lease on the house in which she lives—saved to her by the kindness of some gentlemen who knew her and took some interest in her affairs...."[7] Besides being swindled, Clara may also have lost leases and deeds to her Denver properties in the great Cherry Creek flood in May of 1864.[8]

But as late as May of 1880, Clara was petitioning the Denver City Council for permission to erect a frame building on Lot 27, Block 32 in East Denver. Whether her finances so dramatically declined in a matter of months that she went from being a developer to a charity ward is uncertain; another possible explanation is that the principal reason for her relocation into the Chever house was not so much her finances as her declining health.[9]

Another possible reason could be seen in a small notice in the *Register* of February, 1880. It announced the sale of more of Clara's property, this time along the south side of Lawrence Street. She had originally purchased the lots from Henry Teller, and erected two buildings upon them. In 1870, she issued a deed of trust to Lewis Doll for $500, payable six months later, or to be carried at the interest rate of three percent monthly.[10]

Clara held the properties for a number of years, probably renting them. But in 1880, she went into default and the properties were sold in front of the courthouse on February 28; the price bid was just $425.

Despite the loss, she may have still owned property in Gilpin County. The Central City paper in March, 1881, reported that, "Aunt Clara Brown, one of the old pioneers of Colorado, and who is so favorably known in connection with the colored people of the state, came up from the valley last night, and will remain in Gilpin county some time."[11]

The following year, the notary in one of her land transactions acknowledged that Aunt Clara "appeared before me." But that was just for a quit claim deed for $25.[12] The picture is unclear, but the majority of evidence is that her financial standing had suffered considerably. And she was soon to find herself in quick need of funds.

On a muddy street in Council Bluffs, Iowa, in February of 1882, Clara was reunited with her long-lost daughter Eliza Jane, whom she had not seen in some 47 years. How the reunion was effected, the details of their initial connection and Clara's trip to Iowa, are typically confusing. But we should not let that diminish our appreciation—our wonder!—at this glorious reunification.

For more than forty years, Clara held resolutely to her belief that her daughter was alive, and that she would somehow be united with her. Her travels around the country—to the river towns of Missouri and Kansas, to the gold fields of Colorado, her return to the state where she was separated from her family by sale, her recent relief mission to the southern emigrants to Kansas—can be seen as a constant search for her missing daughter. At one point she had offered a reward of $1000, a year's wages for a workingman, to be proclaimed, and in the *Republican* article that first announced the reunion to the Denver public, it was recorded that "she caused letters of inquiry to be sent all over the country. The case was referred to often in the colored churches of Denver, and every time Aunt Clara met strangers, she entreated them to keep a lookout for her daughter."[13]

86

Her many friends must have thought her obsessed, even slightly mad. Such reunions had been common in the years after the Civil War—freed blacks from Texas and Missouri and Ohio returning for sometimes joyous, sometimes sorrowful discoveries of families torn asunder, some to be reconstituted but many lost forever. But those events must have become fewer and fewer over the 20 years since the war. And Clara's family had been severed nearly 20 years before that!

Certainly Clara's deep and personal Christian faith sustained her hope during those long years of separation. As the same *Republican* article cited above put it, the "old lady is also an earnest Christian, and she has firm faith in the efficacy of prayer. She has never ceased to ask God, whenever she prayed, to restore her daughter to her...."[14] But even she must have started to believe—and her many friends in the churches in Denver and Central City must have counseled—that her reunion with her daughter would come in heaven, and not on this earth. But they were all wrong. For Clara, her life-long prayer truly was answered.

Printed words on a page can but hint at the emotion of this moment, but the reporter of the *Council Bluffs Nonpareil* gave it a determined effort:

> *Yesterday morning, on the Denver Short Line train, Mrs. Brown arrived in Council Bluffs and proceeded to the residence of her daughter. She came up on the street car, and when at the corner of Broadway and Eighth street her long-lost child was pointed out to her, standing on the crossing. With a scream she jumped from her seat, rushed out of the car, and in an ecstasy of joy mother and child were clasped in each other's arms. Unheeding the lookers-on, unheeding the mud in the streets, clasped in each other's arms, they sat down. The sight was one at once amusing and touching. In that embrace the joys and sorrows of a life-time were forgotten, and only the present thought of.*[15]

After Clara, her daughter, and at least one granddaughter returned to Denver, the *Republican* must have received a first-hand account, perhaps from someone traveling with Clara:

> *The meeting of the two is likely to be long remembered by those who witnessed it. The daughter knew by what train her mother would arrive, but had been delayed so that she was a considerable distance from the depot when the train came in. It had been raining and was very muddy, but the mother saw the daughter and the daughter saw the mother and, regardless of sidewalks, they both ran directly towards each other. The collision occurred at a point where the mud was pretty deep, and so overcome with emotion was the daughter that she fell, drawing the mother down with her.*[16]

Few people can hold fast to a dream their entire lives, and then realize it. Aunt Clara Brown was one of those fortunate, special people.

As always with the significant events of Aunt Clara's life, the sketchy newspaper accounts are somewhat contradictory; they also raise some significant questions. The foremost of these is, how did the two become reconnected? The daughter, we know, was Mrs. Eliza Jane Brewer. She returned to Denver with Aunt Clara, and was still living in Denver a few years later. Apparently, she was interviewed by the *Republican* reporter who wrote a lengthy article on Aunt Clara in June 1885. That account of the momentous discovery reads like fiction:

> *There is a romantic story connected with her daughter, Mrs. Eliza Jane Brewer, who now resides in this city. Mrs. Brewer says that some two years ago she was residing in Kansas City and went one day to the post-office, where tickets were on sale for a performance of "Uncle Tom's Cabin."*
>
> *The tickets were in the hands of a Kentucky lady, who, attracted by something familiar in Mrs. Brewer's face, entered into conversation with her, and discovered...that she was connected with the Colorado party, of which Aunt Clara was the head, and with whom the Kentucky lady was well acquainted. One point in the conversation led to another, and after some days when the two met again, the lady expressed a belief that Mrs. Brewer and Aunt Clara were mother and daughter.*
>
> *A letter dispatched to Aunt Clara took her very soon to Kansas City, where sufficient evidence was obtained of the relationship, and mother and daughter were united at last.*[17]

Unfortunately, this account is so riddled with errors that it is hard to take very seriously, and its syntax confuses us further. It reads as though Eliza Jane was connected with "the Colorado party," whatever that means; if it is the wagon train of ex-slaves from Kentucky and Tennessee in 1865, of which it could rightly be said Aunt Clara was the "head," then Eliza had long since vanished by that time. And of course, the other versions of the reconciliation have the reunion taking place in Council Bluffs, not Kansas City, and the fact that one was written in the Council Bluffs newspaper further supports that version—Bruyn also found directories listing Mrs. Brewer as a Council Bluffs resident.

Still, it's a charming story, and a delicious irony—Harriet Beecher Stowe's anti-slavery diatribe occasioning the reunion of two ex-slaves! And it does have support in Clara's obituary, which recounts that Eliza Jane "was discovered in Kansas City two years since by a lady who knew Aunt Clara, and who thought she had traced out the relationship."[18] But as that was in the same newspaper, one suspects that the reporter who wrote the lengthy obituary probably just consulted the earlier piece for background information.

A more likely story is told by the *Republican* article of February 18, 1882, first announcing the news of the discovery.

On Tuesday last Aunt Clara was almost overwhelmed with joy upon the receipt of a letter from Council Bluffs, Iowa, giving tidings of her long-lost daughter, Eliza Jane. The letter was written by a colored woman who formerly lived in Denver, and who was familiar with the story of the old aunty's life. It was some time ago that the woman went away to Council Bluffs, and last week she became acquainted with another colored woman in that city. In conversation it was developed that the woman was none other than Eliza Jane, the long-lost daughter of Aunt Clara Brown. Eliza remembered distinctly about her mother and sisters and brothers, and that she formerly belonged to George Brown of Russellville, Kentucky. When told that her mother was living in Denver, she became almost frantic in the desire to see her, and the letter was written in order to fully verify whether the relationship was true beyond the shadow of a doubt. Aunt Clara was unable to take the matter philosophically, and ever since the letter she has been crying for joy, and thanking God for his goodness in restoring her child to her. A telegram was sent to Eliza Jane at Council Bluffs last night, assuring her that there was no mistake, and that Aunt Clara would come to Council Bluffs as soon as she could perfect the necessary arrangements.[19]

The story goes on to mention that Clara had "no funds to pay her passage, and she is waiting until her friends secure a pass or raise enough money to pay her fare. The old lady has had a half-fare ticket for several years, and if a full pass cannot be secured, her friends will contribute enough to buy a railroad ticket…. The case is one of the most remarkable that have been handed down from the days of slavery, and transportation should be provided for the old mother so that she can leave for Council Bluffs as soon as possible. It is a case worthy the consideration of the charitable people of Denver. If a pass cannot be secured, a contribution should be taken up, so that Aunt Clara may be able to go on her way rejoicing."[20]

The entire story—almost 40 column inches—is at once both a celebration of Aunt Clara's long and noteworthy life, and an appeal for funds or other support. (It was also, it must be recognized, an *amazing* news story.) As a fundraiser it was apparently successful, since upon the return of mother and daughter (and granddaughter!) from Council Bluffs, a short piece entitled "Aunt Clara's Thanks" ran in the *Republican*:

Old Aunt Clara, the colored woman so well known in Central and in this city, wishes to express her thanks to the many friends by whose generosity she has been enabled to meet her daughter, who was sold out of her arms at the age of one and a half years, some forty years ago….

The writer, unacquainted with the facts, found some

difficulty in ascertaining them, but thanks seem due to the Union Pacific Railroad for passes and concessions in fares; to the Central Presbyterian Church through its pastor and deacons for clothing and money; to the Rev. Mr. Clelland and his congregation of Council Bluffs, for the fare of the granddaughter, who returned with Clara and is to make her home with her; and to the Steam bakery for provisions.

It is evident that these, and probably other friends, have contributed greatly to the happiness of both mother and daughter, and that the gratitude of Aunt Clara, at least, is most profound.[21]

Though Aunt Clara hadn't lived in Central City for several years, the local paper there still considered her reunion newsworthy:

Everybody in this section of the mountains knows and respects Aunt Clara Brown. Although her lines have not fallen in pleasant places, her life has had many tinges of romance. Thirty years ago, in the days of slavery, under the peculiar institution, Aunt Clara was separated from a daughter. The war came on, and slaves were freed. Aunt Clara came west, and has done much for her people. A few days ago in Council Bluffs, this good old woman discovered her long lost daughter. Everybody who knows Aunt Clara will rejoice at her good fortune.[22]

Considering the extensive newspaper coverage of Aunt Clara's reunion and her life in Denver for her remaining years, surprisingly little is known about her daughter. The same *Republican* article cited above says that she was "the mother of nine children, of whom she had the principal care, as her husband was parted from her in war times."[23] The paper later wrote that she was "a widow, some 45 years of age."[24]

Another time, the *Republican* had a somewhat more detailed description: "Mrs. Brewer is a widow, apparently some 40 years of age, of very pleasant manner and good appearance. She is wholly devoted to Aunt Clara, and is a daughter of whom any mother might be proud. Like the numerous neices [*sic*], she is quiet and respectful, and seems, as they all do, to regard Aunt Clara as a veritable mother in Israel, whom it is a solemn duty to honor."[25]

Once again we are faced with some apparent contradictions in the reportage. The various writers were either being kind to Mrs. Brewer, or she was being coy with them. If Clara's marriage, when she was 18, was in 1821, and the family was separated after the death of Ambrose Smith in 1835, Eliza Jane was probably about 10—her twin sister, Paulina, died at age eight. But one account says that she was "sold out of her [mother's] arms at the age of one and a half years, some forty years ago." Confusing things further, one article had it that "she formerly belonged to George Brown of Russellville, Kentucky." The pronoun seems to refer to Eliza Jane, not Clara, and all other indications point to her separation from Clara before Clara went to the Brown home. In any case, Eliza Jane was by this time probably in her mid-fifties; some of her nine children may well have married and had children of their own. Aunt Clara was very possibly a great-grandmother!

Again, this will probably never be clear; Eliza herself, like Clara, may not have known when she was born, or where. Similarly, the "neices" referred to were probably some of Clara's numerous friends, who confused the white reporter by their constant references to "Aunt" Clara. But it does seem likely that at least one granddaughter returned with Eliza Jane and Clara, and continued to live with them in the little white frame house on Arapahoe Street.

Chapter 12

However much finding her daughter may have lifted Aunt Clara's spirits, it did nothing for her deteriorating health or financial condition. Indeed, adding two more women to the small household must have further taxed Clara's diminishing savings. But as the tale of the donation of her train fare, as well as Chever's provision of living quarters, both demonstrate, she was well loved, and her many friends now came to her aid.

Most of that aid—no doubt the largest part—was spontaneous and unorganized. But there were also more organized efforts, and they involved some of the most prominent citizens of Colorado.

One of these came in the spring of 1884. By now Clara was physically frail, and seemingly impoverished. A movement to assist her began among some of the most prominent society ladies of Denver. A record of their initial solicitation survived in the files of the Gilpin County Pioneer Association, from whom the ladies sought a contribution for the former Gilpin resident:

> *Denver, March 4, 1884; P.M. Central City. At the request of Mrs. Stimson Smith, one of the committee on a dinner for the benefit of 'Aunt Clara Brown', I write to inquire whether the 'Old Timers' of Central City are engaged in an effort to raise funds for this venerable and worthy woman. We have been informed that such is the case and Mrs. Smith wishes that if so, a communication to that effect might be sent to Mrs. A. J. Jacobs, chairman of our committee, as a means of adding interest to the occasion. This dinner is to be given at the City Hall, Thursday, March 6th. We are very desirous to make it a thorough success, and not knowing whether what we have heard is true regarding this announcement on foot in Central City, address this line to you with the request that you will give it to those who, if we have been correctly informed, have the matter in charge, asking then to communicate at once with Mrs. A. J. Jacobs, 541 Arapahoe St.*[1]

The letter was signed by J. M. Parsons "for the committee." Mrs. A. J. Jacobs was, of course, the same Frances Wisebart Jacobs who would later become known as the founder of the United Way, and doubtless an old friend of Clara's from when Jacobs' O. K. Store operated in Central City. As the address shows, the Jacobs family were also near neighbors of Aunt Clara on Arapahoe Street in Denver.

The ladies' involvement followed an earlier solicitation by Byers' *Rocky Mountain News,* and that article in turn became the source for a piece in the Central City *Register-Call,* under the headline "For Charity's Sake, A benefit for Aunt Clara Brown, one of the Old Pioneers."

> *Yesterday's Denver News contains the following: Some three years ago old Aunt Clara was made the subject of a great deal of newspaper notoriety, on account of her finding a daughter, who had been lost to her for thirty years. None have kept in mind the character and many noble deeds of this poor old '59er to this day, while others who were deeply inter-ested in her case then, have now lost sight of her altogether.*
>
> *Now, through the advice of some of the most promi-nent citizens of Denver, she has decided to ask the kind friends who wish to help her in her need, to attend a dinner party given by her next Thursday, February 28, at 565 Larimer street. The use of this place has been given free of charge by the proprietor, Mr. Peck, who came to Denver in 1860, and his example is a good one to follow. Let those who came in the early days especially see to it that Aunt Clara is richer in her feeble old age for some contribution. Ladies or gentlemen, young or old, who are willing to assist in making arrange-ments for Aunt Clara's benefit, are requested to meet at her lit-tle home, No. 607, Arapahoe street, next Saturday afternoon, at 2 o'clock.*
>
> *While many of the Gilpin county friends of Aunt Clara cannot be present, they will respond liberally to the call, through a handsome purse that will be presented to her that evening.*
>
> *A purse of money is being raised in Gilpin county for the benefit of Aunt Clara Brown, among the old pioneers. Those wishing to contribute will please leave their contribu-tion with Mr. Alfred H. Whitford, Black Hawk, Mr. W. W. Tiffany, at the postoffice, Central, and with Mr. John W. Ratliff, Nevadaville. She is now in very destitute circumstances and is a worthy object of charity.[2]*

The appeal was naturally well received in Central; the same files of the Gilpin County Pioneer Association have a list of contributors that included some of the most prominent business people in the City: Thomas Hooper, the brick-maker; Sam Lorah, city clerk and local agent for the Colorado Central railroad; John C. McShane, of the Sauer-McShane Mercantile; three-term mayor William M. Roworth, now a director of the Colorado National Bank in Denver; Robert S. Haight, long-time police magistrate, justice of the peace, and city clerk in Black

Hawk; Alvin Marsh, an attorney who served as mayor in both Central and Black Hawk, and later became attorney general for the state of Colorado; and many others.

Word of the fund drive had also reached Black Hawk. A petition was circulated, on lined paper, on the top of which was written in purple ink and a beautiful hand: "Black hawk, Feb. 28th, 1884; To the old Settlers aunt Clary Brown being one / Of the old timers and in Need of help / we ask you to contribute to her relief." A list of contributors and the amounts followed.

The event took place as scheduled, and was dutifully reported in the *Republican*:

Aunt Clara Brown was happy yesterday. Wearing a neat calico dress and white apron, with a turban upon her white head, the old lady sat in the lecture room of the City Hall and received all who came to her benefit dinner with a hand shake and warm thanks, and listened with beaming face to their kind words and good wishes.

The interest and cordial sympathy this old colored woman has attracted to her will not be understood by those who do not know something of her past life...some of the ladies of Denver, who were cognizant of the old woman's past history, or who knew her in the early days, determined to have an all-day dinner in the City Hall for yesterday, the proceeds of which would be devoted to her benefit. At the head of the charitable movement were Mrs. A. J. Jenkins [Jacobs?], Mrs. Parsons, Mrs. Joseph Lambert, Mrs. Stimson Smith and Mrs. A.L. Westover, and in their efforts to secure co-operation from the citizens of Denver, they met with very general success. The dinner provided was elegant and substantial, and was served to the large number who came by the fair hands of some of the most prominent society ladies of Denver, the entertainment lasting from early in the afternoon until late at night, the Denver pioneers patronizing the affair liberally.

The Argonauts of Gilpin county remembered Aunt Clara by telegraphing a gift of $25 to her, and received most heartfelt thanks from the beneficiary. The expenses of the ladies were light, and they thought last night, when the feast was declared to be over, that they had made quite a financial success of their benevolent enterprise.[3]

Clara's thanks were expressed in another way, as well. Another of her caretakers during this time was A. G. Rhoads. An early Gilpin businessman, his "Cracker Factory" on Black Hawk Street in Black Hawk shows up prominently in early photographs of that mill town. He later moved to Denver, establishing his Rhoads' Steam Bakery on Fifteenth Street; it was this bakery that provided "provisions" for Aunt Clara's train trip to meet her daughter in Council Bluffs.

Later, Rhoads' operation became part of the National Biscuit Company, now known as Nabisco.

Rhoads was apparently in close contact with Clara, for he wrote on her behalf to the Gilpin County pioneers just the next day:

> *Denver, Colo., March 7, 1884. Sweet William & All the Pioneers; Please allow me on behalf of Aunt Clara & her many friends to express my warmest thanks for your very generous offering of $25 & believe me when I tell you no more heartily appreciated by the dear old girl. God bless the Gilpin Co Pioneers. When my wife broke the news of the $25.00 from your society to Aunt Clara she was "all broke up," and only found relief in having a good cry. The benefit was a success financially and socially. I think the old lady will realize $150.00. "Lord bless you honey by the help of God I am very thankful, yes thank God, thank God, thank God." (Aunt Clara)*[4]

Rhoads also was influential in another organization, which would provide recognition and aid to Aunt Clara in her declining years.

As early as 1866 plans were underway for some sort of organization that would recognize, honor, and to some extent provide care for the earliest pioneers of Colorado. In fact, an earlier organization with newsman William Byers and Levi Russell, brother of early Georgia placer miner William Green Russell, may have existed. But on June 23, 1866, the first recorded meeting of what was to become the Society of Colorado Pioneers took place. The members included: Byers; D.C. Oakes, author of one of the first guidebooks to the Pikes Peak area; Clara's old friend from the first Sunday School meeting in Denver, Lewis Tappan; John Quincy Adams Rollins, founder of Rollinsville in northern Gilpin County; Richard Sopris, later to become mayor of Denver and whose daughter, Indiana, married Gilpin historian Samuel Cushman; and A. G. Rhoads.

The next recorded meeting is in January 1872, with 27 original settlers; another old friend of Clara's, O. J. Goldrick was secretary. By 1877, this group was having annual meetings; Sopris, by now mayor of Denver, was president, with Caleb S. Burdsall 1st vice president, Goldrick secretary, and Central City newspaperman/lawyer D.C. Collier, another old friend of Clara's from the earliest days, another director. At a board meeting at Sopris' office on December 20, 1880, the group made plans for a major reunion and banquet.

The banquet was held in January at the Windsor Hotel. The event was covered in often excruciating detail by the Denver papers; the *Republican* proclaimed that the "first annual reunion and banquet of the Colorado pioneers at the Windsor hotel last evening was an event that will exist in the traditions of the state so long as the memory of Pike's peak and Cherry creek is retained."[5]

A glorious event it may have been, but limited in its scope. The guest list was published in the paper (along with the speeches, the toasts, and the prayers), and though it presented a splendid roll call of the founders of Colorado, conspicuously absent were any people of color. Women were represented only by the repeated "& wife."

Gilpin County pioneers had formed a similar organization, for those who had settled in that historic area in the earliest days.[6] They, too, held an annual banquet, and the *Register-Call* reported that at their January, 1884, meeting at the Teller House, on motion of Thomas Hooper "the secretary was instructed to extend an invitation to Aunt Clara Brown to attend the next banquet."[7]

Clara was apparently well enough at this point to travel to Central City, as the paper, in reporting on the event, noted that among those "coming from a distance were Mr. A. G. Rhoads, and Mrs. Clara Brown, of Denver." She probably traveled on the train under the care of the garrulous Rhoads, but while in Central, "Mrs. Clara Brown—Aunt Clara—while in the city was the guest of Mrs. Henry Poynter. 'Aunt Clara' met with a hearty greeting last evening from all old friends."[8]

Perhaps spurred by the treatment afforded Clara by the Gilpin County group, the Denver pioneers corrected their oversight later that year when Barney Ford and Clara Brown were admitted in September 1884. Clara was the first woman admitted, and obviously the first black woman. It is not known if she attended the banquet that year, but in June of 1885, the association "presented Aunt Clara a check for $50 the other day. She was honestly happy in being thus remembered by her old friends, and expressed herself in no unfeeling terms regarding the Association's kindness."[9]

Clara did, however, attend the September 1885 reunion. She had been "ill off and on for three or four months, but had recovered sufficiently to attend the recent pioneer banquet at the St. James, where she was conveyed in a carriage by members of the association. Aunt Clara was the only female member of the organization. She expressed herself as much pleased with the festivities, and was overjoyed at the treatment she received from her old friends."[10] A later article remembered that she was "scarcely able to sit up," but she insisted on attending.[11] The *Republican* made special note of her presence in a separate short article entitled "A Colorado Pioneer."

> *Aunt Clara Brown, the old colored lady, and the "fifty-niner" whom all the residents of this city at that time knew, the old "aunt" who has nursed so many of them and who has fed not a few when they were hungry and out of cash, was a notable person at the Pioneers' Banquet on Thursday. No lady, young or old, fair or wealthy, had more attention than did she. Wolfe Londoner, in his reply to the toast, to "The Pioneer Women," paid a pleasant compliment to Aunt Clara, and mentioned her as first in the list. He said that Aunt Clara had told him during the evening that she did not know her age within a few months, but that she thought she was 120. He also stated that she had recently been joined by her daughter, who was fifty years old, and from whom she had been separated for forty-two years.[12]*

Sadly, the association would have one last remembrance of Aunt Clara Brown. As early as June, the *Republican* reported that Clara "had been very ill with heart disease of late," and had to be "propped up in her chair."[13] By October 23, the paper felt it necessary to run a short notice that "Old Aunty Brown, a Well-Known Pioneer, Dying in Denver."

> *Information was received yesterday that old Aunt Clara Brown was dying yesterday at her home, No. 607 Arapahoe street, in this city....*
>
> *The Colorado pioneers have always held the old lady in high esteem, and will hear the tidings of her death with the most profound regret.*
>
> *But little hope was entertained last evening that she would survive until morning.*[14]

A few days later, the paper, recounting her 1865 rescue mission to Kentucky and Tennessee, noted somberly that "[t]hese people have ever held Aunt Clara in tenderest rememberance [*sic*]. When the news of her sinking condition reached them, they came to her assistance from various parts of the State, and their tears flowed freely when they realized that the old life which had done so much for them was slowly putting off the burden of years for immortality."[15]

The account continued that '[d]uring the past few weeks she has constantly been growing weaker, and early yesterday her friends saw that she was slipping away."[16] It went on to describe "The Last Scene" in some detail:

> *On the night of her death the scene inside the little cottage on Arapahoe street was solemn and impressive. The room was but dimly lighted, and there was a score of dusky forms seen through the shadows rocking their bodies back and forth, in the manner peculiar to their race, and calling on the Lord, in their strange fashion, for his merciful comfort and assistance.*
>
> *On the bed in one corner, propped up with pillows, lay the aged woman whose strong features, in which the resemblance to her Indian ancestors was plainly visible, were convulsed in their last agony. The gray hair was thrown back from the dark old face, and the tall frame seemed almost that of a giantess. One hand lay outside the coverlet, the other reposed on her heart. Just before the end came she roused herself and tried to speak. The dusky figures gathered round her and strained their ears to listen for her words, but it was in vain. The noble pioneer negress had finished a career of exceptional usefulness and was dead.*

Strangely, yet appropriately, even here—and in the same article!—there is another version of the same tableau. Here it mentions that Jack Smith of Georgetown (mistakenly identified as her brother) was present at her side. More poignantly, it adds:

> *The last time she was conscious she lifted her arms and called out, "Mammy! Mammy!" as if the image of her dead mother was before her.*

In our understandable focus on the miracle of Clara's reunification with her long-lost daughter after so many years, it is easy to forget that Clara herself was the daughter of a slave, that she too was likely ripped away from her mother's arms and sold to strangers. Now, and only now, could Clara be reunited with *her* mother at last.

Just below the lengthy article describing Clara's last hours is a small notice, headed "Attention Pioneers:" "The Society of Colorado Pioneers will meet at City Hall this evening at 7:30 o'clock to attend the funeral of 'Aunt' Clara Brown. The funeral will take place at 10 o'clock tomorrow."

Three days later, there was another article, simply entitled "Aunt Clara Brown." The short piece simply listed a number of "Resolutions Adopted by the Colorado Pioneer Association—Mourning Her Loss." It mentioned that the members of the Committee on Resolutions, who apparently drafted the heartfelt tribute, were J. Goldburg, Richard Sopris, and Colonel John Milton Chivington.

> *WHEREAS, Mrs. Clara Brown, a member of this Association and a pioneer in 1859, having passed to that land where sickness and suffering is not known, and*
>
> *WHEREAS, The philanthropic disposition our dear friend showed by having smoothed the pillow and answered the appeal for help of many a poor sufferer in the days that tried the truest hearts, and*
>
> *WHEREAS, We hold in grateful remembrance the kind old friend whose heart always responded to the cry of distress, and who, rising from the humble position of a slave to the angelic type of a noble woman, won our sympathy and commanded our respect; therefore be it*
>
> *RESOLVED, That we sincerely mourn the loss of this noble woman whose many acts of benevolence made her presence like an angel's visit, and may Heaven amply reward her in the unknown land beyond the range.*[17]

Chapter 13

So who was this woman, who could inspire politicians and hard-boiled military men to such praises, whose passing was worthy of such a dramatic retelling? There's a delightful story related in Isaac Beardsley's history of early Methodism in Colorado, *Echoes From Peak and Plain*, that highlights several aspects of Aunt Clara's character that are worth examining further:

> *One morning about five o'clock she was walking up Eureka Gulch, just above where the Methodist Episcopal church now stands, with a basket of clothes on her head, singing as she strode along under her heavy burden. Taking her load down for a moment, and seating herself to rest, she began clapping her hands and shouting, "Bless the Lord! Bless the Lord! I am so happy this morning." A prominent lawyer, passing just then, hearing her songs of praise and expressions of joy, said to himself, as he walked on, "What is it that makes that colored women so happy? She certainly must have something that I have not." That reflection, after a little, became the means of his conversion.[1]*

This charming little parable, even if apocryphal, tells us much about Aunt Clara. First, it gives us some indication of her physical strength. By the time described, after 1860 but apparently before the completion of St. James Methodist Church in 1872, Clara was in her sixties. Central City is about 8500' in elevation; merely walking at such an elevation up and down the city's numerous hills is a chore for people of any age, much less for the elderly. But Clara walked these hills for two decades, carrying heavy loads of laundry.

Washing clothes was a difficult way to make a living in the 1800's. Clara would have had to gather (or cut and split) her firewood and stoke the fire, haul water, work the heavy miner's clothes against her washboard, wring or hang the wet clothes, and struggle with the heavy flatirons for pressing the clothes. The process was not only difficult, but time-consuming and even dangerous. A "Farmer's Wife" suggested adding chemicals to the laundry in an 1879 article, "How to Make Washing Easy."

> *Fill your tubs two-thirds full of warm water in which you have dissolved one pound best laundry soap. Put in your clothes; add one tablespoonful spirits turpentine and two*

*tablespoonsful spirits of ammonia; agitate the whole for a few
minutes, then spread a heavy sheet or other cloth over the tub
to prevent too rapid evaporation of ammonia and to retain the
heat of the water. Let the clothes remain two hours in the
water; have a folding-bench wringer and wring them into the
rinsing water, then blue them and they are white and clean.*[2]

Aunt Clara did this probably six days a week, throughout her sixties and
seventies. This was in addition to all her charitable work, and the ordinary, but
still demanding, tasks of keeping a house in frontier Colorado.

By all accounts Clara was an impressive physical presence. One writer
declared that she "has been known to travel on foot 25 or 30 miles to care for a
lonely miner who had been taken sick, without receiving a cent."[3] She was
almost universally described as tall, the *Republican* obituary saying that, in
death, "the tall frame seemed almost that of a giantess."[4]

James Thomson, describing her in 1872, pictured her with "good head,
grey hair, good features; wonderful roll of eyes and opening of mouth from
broadest comedy, even when her story most serious."[5] And the *Republican*, pro-
filing Aunt Clara just a few months before her final illness, painted a very similar picture:

> *She is a tall woman, very aged, yet she does not show
> the advance of years, save that she is toothless, and conse-
> quently her conversation is a little difficult to understand. She
> has a remarkable face, with high cheek bones, a long, pointed
> nose and very black eyes. Her cast of features is strong and
> almost classical, and the hair which curls above her temples is
> as white as snow.*[6]

The impressed reporter told Clara that she "must have been a very handsome girl," and wondered if people didn't "always tell you were good-looking?"
Clara admitted that they had. But other portraits, though less flattering, are essen-
tially in agreement. Banker Frank Young, who would have known Clara throughout her stay in Central City, wrote that "her skin is black, her figure lanky, angu-
lar and loose at the joints, and her garments—such as they are—hang from her
shoulders with even less of grace than the empty ones that swing to and fro on
the clothes-line that she fills daily in her never-ending toil. Physically perhaps
you would find few human figures less attractive...."[7]

Many of her facial features seem to have resulted from the combination
of her African-American and Cherokee forebears. So thought the *Republican*
reporter, who wrote that "[t]hus her peculiar cast of face is accounted for; it is
wholly unlike the usual African type, and must impress all who study it with its
singular strength."[8]

Still, none of the accounts anywhere indicated that Clara was thought of
as anything other than a black woman. We have seen how, despite her sense of
Christian unity, she paid particular care to the needs of her fellow African-

Americans, and certainly the scene Beardsley described of Clara carrying a basket of clothes on her head hearkens back to her southern, and ultimately to her African, heritage.

Beardsley's account is the only one we have of her singing, but it is not hard to imagine Clara humming the spirituals she knew as a girl as she walked, or joyously joining in the great hymns of the faith in the various churches she attended. Her voice, given her size, was probably a strong one: Thomson remarked that she "talked capitally."[9]

But it was not how she talked, but what she said that most impressed itself on those who met her. Again, the *Republican* reporter in June, 1885, gave us a clear indication of what a conversation with Clara was like:

> *She replies to all questions put to her in a droll, characteristic way, interspersed with quotations from Scripture and audible blessings to the Lord, whom she considers her safeguard at all times. In fact it is very difficult to get her to talk on any other subject but religion, although she expresses herself intelligently, and some of her ideas are decidedly original.*[10]

The *Republican* interview is laced with Clara's "droll" humor, and Thomson also recorded her affinity for the "broadest comedy." Thomson must have asked her why she never remarried, to which she replied, "[i]f any one would marry me now I wouldn't have him for being such a fool."[11]

And her willingness to repeat Wolfe Londoner's jest regarding her age at the 1885 pioneer banquet[12] to the Central City paper[13] shows a great appreciation for a joke, even when it was on her.

But as the Beardsley vignette shows, it is for her declarations of faith, not her wit, that Clara's conversation was chiefly known. This single-minded devotion caused difficulty for the *Republican* reporter cited above, and it similarly troubled Clara's later biographer, Kathleen Bruyn. In her notes for her 1970 book Bruyn wrote of Clara: "[r]eligious fervor remained almost fanatic, but don't overplay this."[14] But however unsettling this fervor was for her later biographers, a survey of the contemporaneous accounts makes it clear that Clara's Christian faith, however expressed, was the defining characteristic of her life.

Thomson, sharing a coach ride with Clara in 1872, came away with the impression that she spoke with "perfect matter of fact faith."[15] The *Republican* profile, just prior to Clara's reunion with her daughter, mentioned that she was "an earnest Christian, and she has firm faith in the efficacy of prayer. She has never ceased to ask God, whenever she prayed, to restore her daughter to her, and now that the daughter has been found, Aunt Clara is disposed to give all the credit to the Almighty. She is a very pious woman, and is well versed in the Bible. Her belief in religion borders almost upon superstition...."[16]

And a few days later, the reporter with the *Council Bluffs Nonpareil*, after describing the reunion itself, came to a similar conclusion:

Working hard and saving, she never lost faith that she
should again see her child until about three weeks ago. This
woman shows in a remarkable degree that simple and implicit
faith in God which is characteristic of the old slave. In this she
has found consolation for many a sad and lonely hour, her sol-
ace in affliction, and has said to the troubled soul, "Peace, be
still."[17]

Her friend A. G. Rhoads similarly recorded Clara's constant religious declarations, writing to the Gilpin pioneers in 1884: "I saw 'Aunt Clara' last Tuesday eve & took her some grub—she is doing very well this winter—but 'Lord bless you Honey' she is ready to meet her Master—so she states and I presume she is honest in what she says."[18]

The reporter in the June 1885 *Republican* wrote that her "religion is not sectarian,"[19] and so it seemed. She joined the Presbyterian Church in Central City upon its organization in 1862, and apparently kept her membership there, as she was received into the Central Presbyterian Church in Denver by letter of transfer when she moved to Denver in December 1880. But the *Republican* continued, "the various sects around town say that she is always present when their meetings are of any importance. She is a born revivalist, and a great worker in the cause of Christianity."[20]

This lack of doctrinal consistency also troubled Bruyn, who wrote in her notes, "no need to go into her flittings.... But we should have some sort of motivation for her shifts; maybe she jumped in where she thought the need was greatest?"[21] And Clara herself, speaking to the *Republican* interviewer, confirmed that very view: "I go alw'ys whar Jesus calls me, honey," she is reported to have said.[22] In a sketch of Aunt Clara a few years after her death, Hall testified to her "sublime Christian zeal."[23]

Only that kind of deep and personal faith could have sustained Aunt Clara through her long and difficult life, and yet allowed her to come through her experience with no trace of bitterness. The secularist poet James Thomson tried to give her remarkable attitude some philosophical underpinnings; just after quoting her list of deceits and frauds she had suffered, his diary entry continued:

She would rather they treated her so than she them;
which is pure Platonism. They'll have to appear before the
High Court, whose Judge can't be bribed, etc., etc.[24]

But the *Republican* reporter came closer to understanding the fount of her beliefs. After questioning Aunt Clara about her experiences in slavery, he asked:

Wasn't that a dreadful time for you, Aunt Clara?
I thought it was, honey. But oh, chile, jest stop an'
think how our Blessed Lord was crucified. Think how He suf-
fered. My little sufferings was nuthin', honey, an' de Lord He
give me strength to bear up under 'em.[25]

It was her religious faith, then, that guided her "philanthropic disposition;" Bruyn in her notes compared her to Albert Schweitzer, the great Alsatian missionary physician.[26] The same June 1885 *Republican* profile, after describing her belief, continued that "she has always been known for her charitable benevolence. She has spent a great deal of money in relieving the distress of others, and in the early days, when there was a great deal of destitution and suffering, she never hesitated to lend aid to all who were in need of it."[27]

Those words, of course, were echoed in the resolutions by the Colorado Pioneer Association, adopted in Clara's honor upon her death. The Association took care of the funeral arrangements. There was a funeral service at Central Presbyterian Church, in Denver. As Clara would have liked, it was an ecumenical service, with the choir from Zion Baptist Church singing. Reverend E. P. Wells presided; hundreds of people, including scores of the original Colorado pioneers, attended. Her hometown paper, the *Register-Call* of Central City, summarized the lengthy coverage in the *Republican* in fine fashion, under the headline, "Clara Brown's Funeral. Touching Tribute to a Well-Known Pioneer Woman":

> Of the funeral of "Aunt Clara" Brown which occurred from the Central Presbyterian church in Denver yesterday, the Tribune-Republican says that it is seldom that more respect has been paid to the dead than was paid yesterday to the remains of the venerable pioneer negress of whom Colorado had heard so much. The arrangements for the funeral were characterized by a degree of simplicity and good taste.
>
> There were in attendance the Governor, the mayor, and several other prominent dignitaries. The funeral was in charge of the Colorado Pioneer Association, and everything was done with the most scrupulous regard for order and fitness.
>
> The decorations on the coffin were done in lilies of the valley and a bunch of ripened wheat, typical of the noble old life gone on before, reposed at some distance from the flowers on the coffin.
>
> The Pioneers wore knots of crepe on their sleeves, and their solemn demeanor said much for the respect in which they had always held the venerable woman.
>
> The services were conducted by the Rev. E. P. Wells, and enough cannot be said in praise of the simple and yet feeling manner in which the minister set forth the story of "Aunt Clara" Brown's life of tender ministry. In the introduction, he gave an animated sketch of Aunt Clara's life, he having been acquainted with her for a period of seventeen years. He recounted her many struggles in Colorado, her life of labor and self-denial, and the large amount of money she had saved and expended in bringing to Colorado her numerous relatives after

the Emancipation Proclamation had set them free.

He said that she used $5,000 to accomplish this, some of which she borrowed, and all of which she paid back in good time. He said her benevolence was almost unexampled, and likened her noble self-denial unto the sufferings of the Savior.

He said he had been her spiritual adviser for years, and that she had always maintained the same cheerful Christian spirit, never complaining, and experiencing serious adversities from time to time; invariably giving away all she had, and returning anew to her labor with gentle patience.[28]

Interment was at Denver's Riverside Cemetery. The pallbearers represented a cross section of those whose Clara's life had touched. There was a harness maker from Denver, Orris Knapp, who had worked in Central City[29] and probably knew Clara, and a developer, L. W. Cutler, whose Cutler Hall stood at 316-8 Holladay Street; we have no idea how Clara was known to him. The black pioneer Ed Sanderlin was a pallbearer, as was Jack Smith, who had once lived with Clara in Central City and had been present at her death. Caleb Burdsall, a physician who dabbled in ore smelting, may have attended Clara in her final illness. And there was her good friend from Black Hawk days, the baker, A. G. Rhoads.

But this was no means the last honor for Aunt Clara. When the Central City opera house reopened in 1932 as a summer playhouse, Anne Evans (daughter of territorial governor John Evans) thought to recognize Colorado pioneers (and raise funds for the project) by having names of chosen pioneers inscribed into the backs of the hickory bentwood chairs, originally built by Peter McFarlane. A donor could "name" a chair by offering a $100 donation. A chair for Aunt Clara was proposed by none other than the opera's fairy godmother, Ida Kruse McFarlane. It was placed in the Parquet, Row H, Level 1, Seat 6. The opera association published a book giving short biographical sketches of those honored. The sketch for Aunt Clara read, in part:

To the pioneers of Central City, "Aunt Clara" needs no eulogy. The name, "Aunt Clara Brown", calls to mind the dignified, gentle nature of her who bore it. ...

She was deeply religious, and often a miner returning to his shack has seen Aunt Clara alone on the mountain-side, praying for the miners underground. Her character and her good deeds made her one of Central City's most respected and beloved citizens.[30]

About the same time, with the renewed interest in the history of the Central City area, an engraved tablet recognizing Clara's contributions to its building was placed on the wall of St. James Methodist Church. The wording was suggested by Dr. Martin Rist, of Denver's Iliff School of Theology.

Years later, another honor came Clara's way. With the construction of the Colorado State Capitol in the late 1800's, a decision was made to produce portraits in stained glass of 15 of Colorado's prominent men (and one woman, Frances Wisebart Jacobs) who had helped shaped the state's destiny for the building's rotunda. More portraits were added over the years to windows in the House and Senate chambers, and in the 1980's windows honoring six minority leaders were commissioned for the Old Supreme Court Chambers. Clara's striking portrayal—featuring a wagon train, a frontier church, and a broken chain—was one of the six. The window follows a design by noted African-American artist Vernon Rowlette—the original painting hangs in Denver's Black American West Museum.

And still today, Clara's life and good works continue to enlighten and inspire. It is rare to find a book on women in the American West, or African-American women, that does not include at least a mention of Aunt Clara. Aunt Clara has even made an appearance in fiction, as a minor character in two Christian novels set partly in Black Hawk.[31]

Most recently, a decision was made to tell Aunt Clara's story in an entirely new medium. After years of consultation and preparation, the Central City opera association commissioned a distinguished American playwright and a noted composer to prepare a full-length opera of Aunt Clara's life, *Gabriel's Daughter*, for production in the 2003 season.

The composer, Henry Mollicone, had been called "[o]ne of the most distinctive American opera composers"[32] by the *Washington Post* in 1998. Best known to Central City audiences for his short piece, *The Face on the Barroom Floor*, Mollicone has also written works for voice, chorus, ballet, and various chamber orchestras, as well as music for film and television. An orchestral work entitled *A Rat's Tale: The Pied Piper Revisited*, was written in collaboration with playwright William Luce.

Luce is again working with Mollicone as the librettist for the Aunt Clara opera. Luce's greatest success was with a one-woman dramatization of the life of Emily Dickinson, *Belle of Amherst*. Julie Harris (who at one point earlier in her career appeared in *The Lark* at Central City, and had a chair with her name engraved there as well) starred in the Broadway production and won a Tony Award for her performance. Luce has written plays for stage, radio and television productions, as well as the libretto for a musical based on James A. Michener's *Sayonara*.

With such talented craftsmen at work, we can hope that the resulting work will catch some of the spirit of this amazing woman, and introduce a new generation of Coloradans to her life and memory.

Nor have others of Clara's fellow black pioneers been entirely forgotten. Barney Ford, besides being the subject himself of several books and articles, was like Clara honored with a stained glass window at the Colorado capitol. His wife Julia was briefly recognized by being listed in the Denver Social Year Book of 1898; apparently there were objections to having a black woman included, as her listing disappeared the following year. Barney died at St. Joseph's Hospital on December 14, 1902. He is buried, along with Julia and his son, Louis Napoleon Ford, near Aunt Clara in Riverside Cemetery.

Clara's old friend Henry Poynter similarly met with both respect and opposition, though on a less grand scale than the famous Barney Ford. He lived out the remainder of his days in Central City, a hard-working man who, though poor, occasionally found money to invest with Clara, Jeremiah Lee and others of the Central City circle. In 1886, the *Register-Call* noted that an "important mining case in which Jerry Lee and Henry Poynter, two of Central's old and respected citizens are interested, has been reversed. The property in question is located in Clear Creek county, and has been a matter of litigation in the courts for several years. The friends of 'Uncle Jerry' and 'Uncle Henry' congratulate them."[33]

Other news of Poynter was rather more pedestrian, however. County records show he was paid occasionally for sweeping the courtroom, or sawing wood for the clerk's office. He worked for some years as custodian of St. James Methodist Church in Central City, where his efforts occasionally received note:

> *The work of renovating the interior of the St. James M.E. church is drawing to a completion. The carpet in the auditorium is down, and is to be mild—a beauty. It is not the old conventional red, but rather of an old-gold shade. Its effect is pleasing—both warm, mellow, and rich. Mr. Poynter, the old "reliable," did a good job.*[34]

His hard work was not always rewarded, however. In 1889, he was victimized in a particularly cruel fashion:

> *Last evening, between 7:30 and 9 o'clock, the residence of Henry Poynter, on Second High street, was entered by sneak thieves and $102 in money stolen. The parties who did the robbery were well acquainted with the premises, and the circumstances connected with the money stolen. They knew that the family were absent at prayer meeting on Wednesday evening; knew when and how long they would remain away; knew that Mr. Poynter received a few days ago nearly one hundred dollars from the M. E. church as janitor's salary, and had a good idea as to where he kept his money.... Mr. Poynter said he was keeping the money in the house for a few days to meet a note about due, or he would have deposited the money in the bank. No clue to the robbers has yet been obtained.*[35]

A month later, it was reported that "Alexander Howard, a Colored Boy, Arrested for the Larceny of Ninety-five Dollars From the Residence of Henry Poynter on Wednesday Evening, March 20th, 1889.... Henry Poynter is an uncle of young Howard...a portion of the money stolen by Howard had been spent in Black Hawk in the purchase of a new suit of clothes, and in a lavish manner among his female acquaintances...."[36]

Once again, it's likely that the family relationship was mistaken by the white reporter, but for any member of the town's small black community to have abused Poynter's trust and godly habits in such a fashion must have hurt him deeply.

Poynter and his wife had no children; after his death in 1895, his remains were shipped to a sister in Leavenworth. The *Register-Call* eulogized him as being "of a kind disposition and was well liked and highly respected by all with whom he came in contact."[37] A few days later, the paper published the resolutions passed by the Gilpin County Pioneer Association, with which he had long been active:

> *Resolved, That by the death of Henry Poynter, this association has lost a faithful and conscientious member, his widow a kind and affectionate husband, and the community an honest and useful citizen. That we tender our sympathy to the widow in her bereavement, with the assurance that though gone from earth he will not be forgotten, and that all who knew him will keep him in kindly remembrance.*[38]

Neither remembrance mentioned anything about him being a black man; considering the spirit of the times, that may have been the greatest tribute of all.

Jeremiah Lee's family finally moved into the brick mansion on Central City's "Banker's Row," and he lived there until his death in 1904. The color bar was lifted, and his children attended public schools in Central City; John, Alice and Sarah were enrolled at least as early as 1870, and Kate by 1871. Two of the girls sang at Easter services in the Catholic church in 1873, and there were frequent reports of their excellent attendance at the schools.

Lee's life, like Clara's, was filled with triumph and tragedy. He and Emily lost an infant son, Theodore, in April, 1870. In 1889, Edwin Jones, husband of their daughter Sarah, died in Leadville. Jones was born in Virginia, but raised in Massachusetts, coming to Colorado with the New Bedford company of Commander French. He opened a barber shop in Black Hawk with Thomas Townsend, before moving to Leadville where he worked with the Lees' son, John.

Kate Lee married an Englishman, James Luke, in 1890 (Henry Poynter was present as a witness) and again, the young people met with sorrow. By 1894, Luke was working with John Lee and father-in-law Jeremiah in the Silver Creek area, just over the Gilpin County line in Clear Creek County. They were making a fine showing of gold, and had erected a 5-stamp mill for processing the ore, when Luke died of "miner's consumption" in May, 1895. He was only 31.

Alice was also married, to an Albert Halden, and the couple moved to Oberlin, Ohio, perhaps to flee what must have seemed to be a family "curse." Perhaps some of the "daughters" that Clara and Jackson Smith had paid to educate at the college had remained there.

By the time of his death on January 9, 1904, Jeremiah Lee was universally known and respected in both Gilpin and Clear Creek counties. His beautiful home in Central City had become a social gathering place, as when, in 1894, "B. T. Vincent, one of the missionary Methodist clergymen of Gilpin County, paid a visit to former congregations in this city and Black hawk this week. He arrived here Wednesday evening, and after services of a religious character were held at St. James M.E. church, a reception was tendered him at the residence of Mr. and Mrs. Jere Lee, which was largely attended."[39]

But it was Lee's wife, Emily, who was truly mourned upon her passing in 1907:

> The announcement of the death of this estimable and well known lady will carry many a pang of sorrow to the people of Gilpin county and those of other portions of the state who were former residents of this section. No other woman in the mountains was ever held in such high esteem and her services ever in such demand in case of sickness as hers, and the mothers were happy in the thought and confident in the recovery of their dearest ones if only Mrs. Lee could come and take care and administer for them, and there are many to-day who will always remember the kind acts of this lady and ever bless her memory for the good she had accomplished in the many homes where she was summoned. ...sick only ten days ago...death relieved her suffering early yesterday morning, surrounded by her daughter Mrs. Kate Luke and many neighbors and friends who were ever ready to help and administer to her wants.
>
> She was born in Virginia, and at the time of her death had resided in Gilpin County 44 years, coming here shortly after the gold excitement had brought this portion of the state into prominence. Althought [sic] colored, her many acts of kindness and willing assistance in cases of sickness and distress, brought her friends from the people of every walk in life, and many a poor miner and family has had cause to bless her for assistance rendered during the dark days of sickness and sorrow.[40]

Emily and several of their children are buried with Jeremiah Lee at Riverside.

The story of Lorenzo Bowman is even more tragic, however. The account of his death was told in the Georgetown paper of December 29th, 1870:

> On Saturday evening last, December 24th, Lorenzo D. Bowman, while in the act of taking home a revolver which he had borrowed, fell on the ice. The pistol, falling from his pocket, struck on the hammer, which happened to be resting on a cap, and the charge exploded.... We are sorry to say that, owing to Mr. Bowman's advanced age, 52 years, he is not expected to recover. Mr. Bowman is an old prospector and a good citizen.[41]

The paper detailed the injury: Bowman's tibia and fibula were shattered. Dr. Irving J. Pollok, a pioneer physician who located in Georgetown after several years of prospecting in Gilpin and Clear Creek counties, amputated the leg. The article discussed the likelihood that Bowman would die before the paper was distributed, noting the cruel choice between the certainty of "lock-jaw" and the perils of amputation in that era. A later dispatch in the same issue gave the inevitable outcome:

> *Since writing the article relating to L. D. Bowman, the unfortunate man has died. He never recovered from the shock given by receiving the wound, and his case was from the first a doubtful one. He died on Monday evening last about 10 pm. Mr. Bowman was a good citizen, and his loss will be greatly deplored by his friends.*

Taking the newspaper account at face value, the story is sad enough; reading between the lines, though, it becomes even sadder. More than a century later, too many "accidental" shootings of black men have been exposed as something other for us to be comfortable with this one. The fact that Bowman's happened on a Saturday night, on a holiday weekend, and with a "borrowed" revolver, is certainly enough to make us suspicious.

Even more, it appears that Bowman had just come into a large sum of money. Just a few days earlier, the Central City paper reported that "the O. K. lode in Georgetown, has been sold to some Baltimore parties, for the sum of $25,000 cash. This lode was formerly owned by Bowman & Co., who gave Judge Cowles & Sons one-half of the mine for developing. While at this praiseworthy work, Cowles & Co. demonstrated that the lode would pay largely. This stirred up Bowman & Co., with the result that the two companies have netted, to date, some $10,000 from this mine."[42]

Certainly we have now no way of knowing the truth of the shooting. Such accidental discharges were not at all uncommon—in fact, the son of Georgetown politician (and one-time partner with Bowman), William A. Hamill, died in 1889 when, while hunting mountain lion at a ranch near Hayden, his rifle was knocked over by a horse and fired a random, fatal shot. The fact that Bowman apparently lingered for some hours after the shot would lead us to hope that he would have had time to tell his account of the event, if it was something other than accidental. Still, his death was a great loss for the black community—and for all Colorado. "We understand that he has no family," concluded the *Register*, "but a host of friends will mourn his loss."[43]

Jennie Spriggs, the black laundress who arrived in Black Hawk about the same time Clara settled in Central City, lived well into the twentieth century; some Black Hawk "old-timers" recall her well. At some point, she took up with a white man named Ed Golden (or Golding), and sometimes used his name. She continued her laundry service in Black Hawk, however, even after the arrival of a number of Chinese-operated laundries; a Jennie "Sprague" is listed in an 1884-85 business directory, for example (along with Lee Min, Lee Wee, and Lee Sang,

Sang Law and Sam Wan in Central City).

Unfortunately, Jennie had made a poor choice in Ed Golden. The papers over the following years are replete with tales of his shady dealings, tales which usually mentioned Jennie, if not always by name:

> *A specimen of humanity, named Ed Golding, who is said to be married to a negress in Black Hawk, who goes by the name of Black Jenny, last Saturday came into the possession of baggage checks belonging to two Colorado women of Boulder, visitors to the city of Quartz mills. Golding secured the baggage and left it in pawn at a saloon near the toll gate. For this breach of faith he was arrested and brought before Judge Samuel H. Bradley, who fined him $12 and costs, in default of the payment of which he now languisheth in the City cooler.*[44]
>
> *Ed Golden, a drunken worthless wood-chopper, last evening entered the store of Mr. William Cochrane in Black Hawk in a hilarious state of mind, and was told that his company was not wanted. To this he objected, when the proprietor collared him and shoved him into the street. Golden whipped out a pocket-knife and opening the big blade made a pass at the bay window of Cochrane, the blade of the knife cutting the leg of his pantaloons. Before Golden could proceed with his attempted dissection of Cochrane, the latter planted his left duke on the back of Golden's neck, knocking him out of time. An officer was summoned and he was landed in the cooler where he remained until this morning.*[45]
>
> *Ed. Golden, the man who attempted to let a little light into the "bay window" of William Cochrane last Monday evening in Black Hawk, was let out of the calaboose yesterday morning, and immediately left the city for his wood camp, where he sought comfort in reclining on the bosom of his dusky maiden, who is known as the "Swamp Angel."*[46]
>
> *Ed. Golden last Saturday was committed to the county jail for ten days by Judge Tonking, of Black Hawk. His crime was that of the larceny of a buck-saw, which he claimed that he had left for sharpening at a carpenter shop. The testimony showed that he pawned the purloined saw for the paltry sum of twenty-five cents and a drink of beer. Rather an expensive saw for Golden, whose greatest crime is that of paying too much attention to a buxsom [sic] colored woman, whose best man he is.*[47]

Later in life, however, Jennie realized the error of her ways. A much-later *Denver Post* newspaper article on Jennie recognized her services as a midwife in the area. Many of these children, long since grown, honored Jennie upon her death in 1921 with a satin-lined casket and a tombstone in Black Hawk's Dory Hill cemetery, an upright piece of sandstone fashioned by Billy Hamilton. A copper door on the headstone opened to reveal a picture of Jennie; but vandals stole the door and the picture, and they have yet to be replaced. An inscription inside read:

> *Dear Friend:*
> *The sun hath seen thee toil*
> *With tired back and brown arms bent,*
> *Though other hands now work and moil,*
> *Thy work is done, go Home content. –Woodbury Lowrey.*
> *She hath done what she could—Mark 14:8.*[48]

Even Aunt Clara herself could not rest peacefully. More than 10 years after her death, her body was exhumed and reburied, in one of three spaces in a lot purchased by Harriet Mason. The reburial took place on January 10, 1896. According to Bruyn, the request for Clara's reburial, and the funds to accomplish it, were contained in the will of this Harriet Mason, whom she believed to be the widow of Andrew Mason.

Andrew Mason was an early Colorado miner; he is named as the manager of the Equatorial Mine in Georgetown in 1869,[49] and was present at the first meeting of the historic Nevadaville Masonic Lodge #4. He moved to South Dakota, and died at Deadwood in 1877.

In her 1970 biography of Aunt Clara, Bruyn was puzzled by this, and wrote that "why Harriet Mason felt so strongly about Aunt Clara was never revealed."[50] Certainly Clara's kindness to people of all races could have touched this Mason family, in ways that would probably never be discovered. But there's no citation in Bruyn's extensive notes, nor any hint in the records of the cemetery, that would indicate that the Harriet Mason who had Clara reburied was in any way related to the Andrew Mason mentioned above. And quite obviously, the instructions for the reburial weren't in Harriet Mason's will, as the reburial took place 10 years before Harriet Mason's death.[51]

The marker adjoining Clara's reads simply, "Harriett I. Mason, 1852-1906." Given the vagaries of census data, could this not be the same Harriet Mason who was listed in the 1870 census as being 21 years old, and was more than likely one of the "orphans and relatives" Clara brought back during her post-Civil War rescue mission from Kentucky? Making this scenario even more likely, there is one other person buried in the plot with Harriet Mason and Clara—Jackson Smith, sometimes mentioned as a brother to Clara and one of the refugees brought back to Colorado in that same rescue mission.

Harriet and her husband, Talton, had numerous business dealings with Clara throughout the 1870's, with Harriet actually buying two lots in Central City[52] from Aunt Clara as late as the summer of 1879. Talton's was one of the six names (along with Jack Nelson Smith) listed on the Location Certificate for the "Aunt Clara" lode in 1870; his name appears directly below Clara's. Surely this woman—one of the closest of the extended "family" that grew up around Clara in Central City in the 1860's and 1870's—would have had more than ample reason for this posthumous recognition.[53] Harriet Mason would have owed her new life in Colorado—her home, her very family—to Aunt Clara and her philanthropy.

The confusion regarding this last honor to the late Aunt Clara Brown is typical, illustrating the difficulties of knowing any detail of her life with any certainty. But at the same time it demonstrates again how wide, and how strong was her influence. Born on the cusp of the 18th century, through her life and character she created a legacy that endures into the 21st. It is a legacy to be treasured, yes, and honored. But, as Clara would surely be the first to remind us, it is a legacy to be lived.

Notes

Chapter 1

1   Preface, *History of Clear Creek and Boulder Valleys, Colorado*. (Chicago: Baskin & Co., 1880) The book also included a sketch of another woman, pioneer naturalist Martha Maxwell, in the Boulder County biographies.

2   Burrell, James, *History of Clear Creek and Boulder Valleys, Colorado*. (Chicago: Baskin & Co., 1880) 443.

3   *Denver Republican*, February 18, 1882.

4   *Denver Republican*, October 27, 1885.

5   Quoted in Randall Clippings, Vol. I, 25-6

6   *Weekly Register-Call*, September 29, 1885. Clara, however, was merely reporting on a jest made by Wolfe Londoner, later Mayor of Denver, at the Colorado Pioneer banquet a few days before.

7   *Denver Republican*, June 26, 1885.

8   The headstone, however, is probably not the original, given the unusual circumstance of her reburial in another plot 10 years after her death.

9   Note however that in a book co-authored by Dr. Noel, *Colorado Givers*, Noel (or one of his co-authors) writes on page 13 that Clara was born in 1800, and in Virginia. That a historian of Dr. Noel's caliber appears uncertain about the circumstances of Aunt Clara's birth demonstrates just how intractable the problem really is.

10   *Colorado Heritage News*, July, 1987.

11   Fitzgerald, Ruth Coder, *A Different Story: A Black History of Fredericksburg, Stafford, and Spotsylvania, Virginia* (Greensboro, N.C.: Unicorn, 1979) 169.

12   Coleman, J. Winston, *Slavery Times in Kentucky* (Chapel Hill: University of North Carolina Press, 1940) 5-6.

13   The account in the *Denver Republican*, February 18, 1882 is particularly garbled, but still gives Ambrose Smith as the first named owner.

14   Burrell, 443.

15   Kolchin, Peter, *American Slavery* (New York: Hill & Wang, 1993) 96-97.

16   Bruyn, Kathleen, *'Aunt' Clara Brown* (Boulder: Pruett; 1970) 3-13.

17   Coleman, 45.

18   Kolchin, 245.

19   Kolchin, 100.

20   *Denver Republican*, June 26, 1885.

21   Bruyn papers, DPL/WHC. Letter from Edward Coffman dated 3/5/62.

22   Coleman, 77-8.
23   *Denver Republican*, February 18, 1882.
24   *Denver Republican*, February 18, 1882.
25   Coleman, 58.
26   Coleman, 120.
27   Bruyn, 4.
28   Coleman, 33.
29   Coleman, 275.
30   Coleman, 275.
31   Thomson, James, *Diary*, Saturday, May 18, 1872.

Chapter 2

1   Bruyn papers, DPL/WHC. Letter from Edward Coffman dated 2/10/65.
2   Bruyn papers, DPL/WHC. Letter from Edward Coffman dated 2/7/65.
3   Bruyn papers, DPL/WHC. Letter from Edward Coffman dated 2/7/65.
4   Bruyn papers, DPL/WHC. Letter from Edward Coffman dated 2/10/65.
5   *Denver Republican*, June 26, 1885.
6   *Denver Republican*, June 26, 1885.
7   Bruyn papers, DPL/WHC. Letter from Edward Coffman dated 2/14/62.
8   Finley, Alex C., *History of Russellville and Logan County* (Frankfort: University of Kentucky.) 24 ff.
9   *Denver Republican*, February 18, 1882.
10   Burrell, 443.
11   Thomson, *Diary*, Saturday, May 18, 1872.
12   *Denver Republican*, March 17, 1890.
13   Hall, Frank, *History of Colorado* (Chicago: Blakely Printing Company, 1889) 483.
14   Burrell, 443.
15   Coleman, 105.
16   *Denver Republican*, February 18, 1882.
17   The clippings of Jesse Randall, pioneer newspaperman in Georgetown, Colorado, contain a curious reference that Clara "escaped to Arkansas." No other evidence supports that route, however. Randall Clippings, Vol. 1, 37-38.
18   Bruyn, 1-2.
19   *Denver Republican*, February 18, 1882.
20   Burrell, 443.
21   Monahan, Doris, *Destination: Denver City* (Athens, Ohio: Swallow Press, 1985) 43.

Chapter 3

1   Willison, George F., *Here They Dug the Gold* (New York: Brentano's, 1931) 8.
2   Hollister, Ovando, *The Mines of Colorado* (Springfield, Mass.: Samuel Bowles & Company, 1867) 8.
3   Willison, 8

4   Willison, 5.

5   Willison, 13.

6   Willard, James F., "Spreading the News of the Early Discoveries of Gold in Colorado," *Colorado Magazine,* XII, no. 1 (Jan. 1935), 99.

7   Paul, Rodman Wilson, *Mining Frontiers of the Far West, 1848-1880* (New York: Holt, Rinehart and Winston, 1963) 111.

8   Rogers, James Grafton, *Rush to the Rockies* (Denver: State Historical Society of Colorado, 1957) 21-2.

9   Cushman, Samuel and J. P. Waterman, *The Gold Mines of Gilpin County* (Central City: Register Steam Printing House, 1876) 19.

10   Cushman, 21.

11   Paul, 111.

12   Goode, Rev. William H., *Outposts of Zion, with Limnings of Mission Life* (Cincinnati: Poe & Hitchcock, 1864) 402.

13   Cannon, Carl L, in Villard, Henry, *The Past and Present of the Pikes Peak Gold Regions* (Princeton: Princeton University Press, 1932) vi.

14   Hafen, LeRoy, *Pike's Peak Gold Rush Guidebooks of 1859* (Philadelphia: Porcupine Press, 1974) 84-5.

15   Burrell, 443.

16   Goode, 402.

17   Hafen, LeRoy R., and Ann W. Hafen, eds., *Reports from Colorado: The Wildman Letters 1859-1865* (Glendale, Ca.: The Arthur H. Clark Co., 1961) 18.

18   Bruyn papers, DPL/WHC.

19   Thomson, James, Letter of February 8, 1872, quoted in Salt, H.S., *The Life of James Thomson ("B.V.")* 72-3.

20   Reyburn, Marjorie, "James Thomson in Central City," *University of Colorado Studies*, Vol. 1, No. 2 (June 1940) 184.

21   Spence, Clark C., *British Investments and the American Mining Frontier, 1860-1901* (Ithaca, N.Y.: Cornell University Press, 1958) 5.

22   Reyburn, 184.

23   Thomson, *Diary,* entry of May 18, 1872.

24   Burrell, 443.

25   Hafen, LeRoy R., "The Last Years of James P. Beckwourth," *Colorado Magazine* 4 (August, 1928) 137.

26   Wilson, Elinor, *Jim Beckwourth* (Norman: University of Oklahoma, 1972) 169.

27   By 1864, when Beckwourth lived on a ranch outside of Denver, he was "married" again to another Indian woman. Wrote Hafen, "[w]hat became of the girl Beckwourth married in 1860 is not clear." Hafen, "The Last Years of James P. Beckwourth," 138.

28   Davis, Herman S., ed., *Reminiscences of General William Larimer* (Lancaster, Pa.: New Era Printing Co., 1918) 208-9.

29   Willison, 102. A slightly different version appears in the *Rocky Mountain News*, Apr. 21, 1968, in an article by Marjorie Bennett, "Negro in Colorado: Proud

History," p. 8-10. Apparently the old frontiersman called all his wives "Lady Beckwourth."

30 *Weekly Register-Call*, August 5, 1921.

31 The original article appeared in the newspaper's *Empire* Magazine, written by Alice Spencer Cook; it was later rewritten as Coleman, Alice, "Jennie Would Like That," *Lakewood Sentinel*, November 8, 1973.

32 A source for the original story was apparently Black Hawk resident Billy Hamilton, who knew Jennie as a young man. Later the caretaker for the Opera House and Teller House in Central City, Billy was known as a "character," a "trickster," and "the biggest liar in Colorado." (Virbick, Diane R, *Denver Post*, May 22, 1981.) This may explain the unlikely version of Jennie's migration to Colorado.

Chapter 4

1   Burrell, p. 443.

2   *Denver Republican*, February 18, 1882.

3   Leonard, Stephen J. and Thomas J. Noel, *Denver: Mining Camp to Metropolis*, (Niwot: University of Colorado Press, 1990) 9.

4   Quoted in Hafen, LeRoy, *Colorado Gold Rush: Contemporary Letters and Reports 1858-1859* (Philadelphia: Porcupine Press, 1974) 331.

5   Diary of E..N. H. Patterson, June 1859, published in *Ogwauka Spectator*, August 18, 1959. Quoted in Hafen, *Overland Routes to the Gold Fields, 1859, from contemporary diaries* (Philadelphia: Porcupine Press, 1974) 185-6.

6   Adriance diary, August, 1859.

7   Winne, Peter, "Historical Gleanings," *The Trail*, Vol. VII, No. 3 (August, 1915) 5-17.

8   *Rocky Mountain News*, November 3, 1859.

9   Quoted in *The Trail*, IV, Jan. 1912, 24.

10 Bruyn, 37 ff.

11 Beardsley, Isaac Haight, *Echoes from Peak and Plain* (Cincinnati: Curtis & Jennings, 1898) 358.

12 Tappan also is given credit for being one of the first white men to visit, and provide the name for, the spectacular rock formations near Colorado Springs known as "Garden of the Gods."

13 Zamonski, Stanley W. and Teddy Keller, *The Fifty Niners* (Denver: Sage Books, 1961) 57.

14 Burrell, 444.

15 Burrell, 444.

16 Burrell, 444.

17 Granruth, Alan, *Mining Gold to Mining Wallets: Central City, Colorado, 1859-1999* ([Central City: Gilpin Historical Society], 1999) 10, 114. The house is now covered with clapboard siding, but was originally a rough-hewn log cabin.

18 Monroe, "Chocolate" Dan, in Granruth, Alan, *The Little Kingdom of Gilpin* ([Central City]: Gilpin Historical Society, 2000) 130.

19 Monroe, 130.

20 Burrell, 245.

21 Quoted in Dunn, William R., *"I Stand by Sand Creek"* (Ft. Collins: Old Army Press, 1985) 40.

22 Zamonski, 154.

23 *Denver Republican*, June 26, 1885.

24 *Denver Republican*, June 26, 1885.

Chapter 5

1 Goode, 428.

2 Hollister, 105.

3 *Miner's Register*, January 14, 1869.

4 Burrell, 443.

5 Burrell, 443.

6 Bancroft, Caroline, *Gulch of Gold* (Boulder: Johnson Publishing Co., 1958) 217.

7 Descriptions of the buildings and businesses of Mountain City can be found in Donald Kemp's *Colorado's Little Kingdom*, Judge Louis Carter's *Yesterday Was Another Day*, and Muriel Sibell Wolle's *Timberline Tailings*, in which she relies on the recollection of Clarence Reckmeyer. Carter notes that the "business section of Mountain City was located on Lawrence Street," which is where Clara's home and laundry are said to have been located. Unfortunately, none of the descriptions mentions her property specifically. Lawrence Street also continued into Central City, becoming Eureka Street at the intersection with Main Street. Generally, Lawrence and Gregory streets parallel the gulch, with Lawrence on the north side and Gregory on the south.

8 Kemp, Donald C., *Colorado's Little Kingdom* (Golden: Sage Books, 1949) 39.

9 Gregory District Record Book D, p. 259.

10 Gilpin County Record Book 38, p. 579.

11 In a 1954 map drawn by Clarence Reckmeyer for amateur historian Muriel Sibell Wolle and included in her second "ghost town" book, *Timberline Tailings*, there is the following inscription: "Now Gregory St., was perhaps first named Bench or California St." But the descriptions of the other properties would suggest a hillside rather than a gulch location. Two fine pictures of early Mountain City are included by Kemp in his book, which identify a number of buildings, but none of them seem to be structures referenced in these documents.

12 The City of Black Hawk is now "recreating" a collection of buildings as Mountain City Historic Park. A few, including a two-story commercial building on Gregory Street and a barn above, are on their original lots. The others are residences which have been moved onto the site. Currently, the restored buildings are being used for City offices.

13 Central City District Record Book A, p. 115.

14 Fell, James E., *Ores to Metals* (Lincoln: The University of Nebraska, 1979) 4.

15 Hafen, *Reports from Colorado: The Wildman Letters* 109; quoting letter of A.F. Garrison, July 4, 1859.
16 Hafen, *Reports from Colorado: The Wildman Letters* 133-5, quoting letter of Rufus E. Cable, July 30, 1859.
17 Hafen, *Reports from Colorado: The Wildman Letters* 166-8, quoting letter in *Missouri Republican*, dated August 28, 1859.
18 Sayre, Hal, "Early Central City Theatricals and Other Reminiscences," *Colorado Magazine,* VI, No. 1 (Jan. 1929) 53.
19 Willison, 72.
20 Axford, William H., *Gilpin County Gold* (Chicago: Swallow Press, 1976) 27-8.
21 Quoted in Willison, 39.
22 Quoted in Smith, Duane A., *The Birth of Colorado* (Norman: University of Oklahoma Press, 1989) 73.
23 Rogers, 17.
24 Goode, 438.
25 West, Elliott, "Women of the Rocky Mountain West," in Smith, Duane A. (ed.), *A Taste of the West* (Boulder: Pruett, 1983)148.
26 Kemp, 44.
27 Goode, 438.
28 Goode, 433.
29 Burrell, 249.
30 *Weekly Miner's Register*, Feb. 19, 1867.
31 Burrell, 239.
32 Burrell, 239.
33 Fiester, Mark, *Look for Me in Heaven* (Boulder: Pruett; 1980) 178
34 Fiester, 248
35 Leyendecker, Liston E., *Washington Hall* [Ft. Collins]: Colorado State University Cooperative Extension Service, [n.d.] 4.
36 Hall, 483.
37 Burrell, 443.
38 Goodykoontz, Colin, "Colorado as Seen by a Home Missionary" *Colorado Magazine*, XII, No. 2 (March 1935) 65; Crawford letter of November, 1863.
39 Gilpin County Record Book 46, p. 379.
40 Goode, 428
41 Hollister, 21.
42 Quoted in Smith, "My Profit, Your Land," in Smith, Duane A., ed., *A Taste of the West.* (Boulder: Pruett, 1983) 101.
43 Hollister, 142-3.
44 Arps, Louisa Ward, "The Gravity Tram of Gilpin County" *Denver Westerners' Roundup* Vol. XXV No. 1 (January 1969) 3-17.
45 Cushman, 45.
46 Peterson, Richard H., *Bonanza Kings* (Norman: University of Oklahoma Press, 1991) 117.

47   Cushman, 7.

48   Goodykoontz, Crawford letter of July 13, 1863.

49   Axford, 28.

50   Guerin, Elsa Jane, *Mountain Charley* (Norman: University of Oklahoma Press, 1968) 55.

51   Goode, 438.

52   Smith, *Birth of Colorado,* 133.

53   *Denver Republican*, March 17, 1890.

54   *Denver Republican*, October 30, 1885.

Chapter 6

1   Hill, Alice Polk, *Tales of the Colorado Pioneers* (Denver: Pierson & Gardner, 1884) 362.

2   Burrell, 443.

3   *Denver Republican*, February 18, 1882.

4   Smith, *Birth of Colorado,* 132. On the other hand, Reverend Adriance, in his Diary, notes that he hired a house from a Mrs. Wilson for $7 a month. Either the complainers cited by Smith were exaggerating their plight, Mrs. Wilson gave Adriance a greatly reduced rate, or rents fluctuated wildly in Central City. Since other prices and wages remained relatively stable, as cited in a number of sources, the explanation may lie in the boom-and-bust cycles that were already plaguing the mining industry. There is one known example of Aunt Clara as a landlord; in 1870 county records show that she was paid $24 a month for use of a house for some paupers, the Tittle family.

5   *Daily Central City Register*, March 26, 1873.

6   Entry of May 18, 1872, quoted in Reyburn, 187.

7   Gilpin County Record Book 44, 142.

8   Coleman, 78.

9   U.S. Bureau of the Census, *Negro Population in the United States, 1790-1915* (Washington, D.C.: Government Printing Office, 1918) 43-4. It's worth remembering that some of those identified in the 1860 census may have been slaves. "Two black slaves toiling at the sluices are pointed out to Ryan by his Georgia friends who inform him of others in the gulch." Willison, 66.

10   Dr. Noel, in his webpage on Ford in the City of Denver website, has him born in 1822 in South Carolina; another webpage on Ford, from the Afro-American Almanac, says he was born in Virginia in 1824.

11   In the Bruyn papers, DPL/WHC, there is a "resume" of a phone conversation she had with Parkhill, on Jan. 29, 1969. She noted cattily that by this time the famed western writer was openly writing history with one eye always on the motion picture possibilities. A juvenile biography by Marian Talmadge and Iris Gilmore, *Barney Ford: Black Baron*, was published in 1973 and would not have been available to Bruyn, though it has similar flaws.

12 Stiff, Cary, "Barney Ford: From Slavery to Riches," *Denver Post, Empire Magazine*, August 3, 1869, 21. Though brief, this seems to be by far the most factual treatment of Ford.

13 *Rocky Mountain News*, quoted in Stiff, 21. The account continues, "[l]ater they were forced upon the hill which was thought to be barren, but, after a brief interval, it turned out to be immensely rich, and the derisive term (Nigger Hill) which was applied to the locality was adopted as a honorable cognomen." Stiff continues, editorially, "'Honorable cognomen' or not, the name 'Nigger Hill' was dropped from local maps and Barney Ford's name was substituted by the Board of Geographic Names."

14 Randall Clippings, July 1903.

15 "His memory is still very retentive, and he delights in relating the incidents of his youth and his travels. His eyesight is also remarkably good, as he reads the **copy of this sketch** without the aid of glasses." (Emphasis added) The remainder of the biographical material on Lee is also from the Randall Clippings.

16 Some accounts say that Lee was a slave of Robert E. Lee, but was given his freedom. For example, see Pearce and Pfaff, *Guide to Historic Central City and Black Hawk*, 34.

17 Randall Clippings, July 1903. The material on Bowman is mentioned in passing in the biographical sketch of Lee, and indicates how closely the two were linked together.

18 *Register*, Sept. 13, 1866. Still another account, by Aaron Frost in the same *History of Clear Creek and Boulder Valleys* that includes Burrell's section on Gilpin County, has it that "Bowman & Company, a party of Negroes from Missouri, were first seized with the smelting mania, and built, in 1865, on Leavenworth Fork, a mile above Georgetown, what is known as the 'Nigger Smelter.' With a rude waterwheel, bellows and ten-foot stack, they reckoned on melting the silver and lead down as easily as they had the 85 per cent galena back in the east. Their mine, the Argentine, furnished a few charges of antimonial galena, but, when they had dug out two or three adamantine 'sows,' the negroes concluded to quit the smelting business, sadder but wiser men. Next came Caleb S. Stowel [*sic*], with a Scotch hearth, which had no better luck." (p. 342) A third version, in David S. Digerness' *The Mineral Belt* (162-63) seems to rely on the reporting of Jesse Randall and is more complimentary to Bowman's contributions.

19 Gilpin County Record Book 30, 121.

20 Randall Clippings, July 1903.

21 He was at one point, for example, 1/3 owner, with Bela Buell and Thomas Richman, of lots 8 and 9 in block 2 in Central City, property later sold to legendary sheriff Dick Williams.

Chapter 7

1 Cushman, 42-3.

Notes

2   Spring, Agnes Wright, *Colorado Charley* (Boulder: Pruett, 1968) 14.

3   Vickers, W.B., *History of Clear Creek and Boulder Counties*, 24.

4   Cushman, 47.

5   Crawford, letter of Feb. 13, 1864, in Goodykoontz, 67.

6   Cushman, 43.

7   King, Joseph E., *A Mine to Make a Mine* (College Station, Texas: Texas A&M University Press, 1977) 11.

8   Smith, *Birth of Colorado*, 159.

9   Hollister, 122.

10   King, 154.

11   Crawford letter of April 12, 1864, in Goodykoontz, 67.

12   Leyendecker, *Bela Stevens Buell* (Denver: University of Denver, 1966) 98-9.

13   Leyendecker, *Bela Stevens Buell* 126; quoting *Rocky Mountain News*, August 26, 1865.

14   Quoted by Smith, *Birth of Colorado* 161-2.

15   "Or what of that numerous class of company's agents, the 'jolly dogs'—usually nephew of the president, or son of the head director—excellent masters of the billiard cut, with uncommon pride in high boots and spurs, whose champagne bills were charged to 'candles' and whose costly incense to Venus appeared on the books as 'cash paid for mercury'? It was a charming farce to witness a General Fitz John and staff of assistants, all finely mounted, reviewing the corps of masons on the stone 'folly,' or riding to and from the mine; but was it business?" (Cushman, 47.) The "General Fitz John" was General Fitz-John Porter, a cashiered Union general who was sent out to Colorado by his admirers after his discharge as local manager for the Gunnell Mining and Milling Company. Though generally competent as a manager, he stumbled badly in building a huge stone mill along lower Clear Creek, then had to sell the milling equipment when it arrived because the company was unable to pay the shipping charges. The building—estimates of its costs ranged up to $200,000—was abandoned. Later, entrances were blasted through either end of the building, and it served as a covered train station when the Colorado Central railroad reached Black Hawk in 1872.

16   Leyendecker, *Bela Stevens Buell* 100-1; quoting Central City *Miners' Register*, April 22, 1864.

17   Smith, *Birth of Colorado,* 156.

18   Quoted in King, 23.

19   Smith, *Birth of Colorado*, 203.

Chapter 8

1   Murphy, Richard W., *The Nation Reunited* (Alexandria, Va.: Time Life Books, 1987) 26.

2   The Thirteenth Amendment, outlawing slavery, was passed by Congress January 31, 1865, but not ratified by a two-thirds majority of the states until December 6 of that

year. The Fourteenth Amendment, guaranteeing equal rights regardless of race, passed Congress on the same date, but languished until July of 1868. In the interim, the Civil Rights Act of 1866 was passed.

3   Robinson, Cedric J., *Black Movements in America* (New York: Routledge, 1997) 87.

4   Kolchin, 241.

5   *Rocky Mountain News*, August 7, 1866.

6   Burrell, 443.

7   Thomson, *Diary,* entry of May 18, 1872.

8   *Denver Republican*, February 18, 1882.

9   Hall, 483.

10   *Denver Republican*, February 18, 1882.

11   Letter dated January 23, 1969; Bruyn papers, DPL/WHC. Also in the papers is an advertisement for the Missouri Pacific, quoting a St. Louis to Leavenworth fare of $9. As that distance is 309 miles, that is a rate of just under three cents a mile. But, as Castner noted in his letter, "[r]ail fares immediately after the War varied from 3-4 cents a mile on Northern and Midwestern lines to 4-6 cents and higher on Southern lines." His use of the five cent figure was a rough approximation.

12   Letter dated January 23, 1969; Bruyn papers, DPL/WHC.

13   Atkins, Joseph, *Human Relations in Colorado* (Denver: Colorado State Department of Education, 1961) 15.

14   Bruyn papers, DPL/WHC.

15   If the writer was indeed Gilpin-based, he would only have been aware of those emigrants who came to the area. If others remained in Denver, as Burrell specifically mentions, this could also explain the smaller number—16—used in the *News* article.

16   Perkin, Robert L., *The First Hundred Years* (Garden City, N.Y.: Doubleday, 1959) 34. This Jack Smith married Mary Mack in October, 1865. (*Rocky Mountain News,* Oct. 18, 1865.) It is worth noting that Jesse Randall, in his Clippings, says that the other Jack (Jackson) Smith, who attended Clara at her deathbed, was a brother. Given the undoubted familiarity with which members of Colorado's early African-American community addressed each other, it seems unlikely that he was a literal blood relative. Randall Clippings, Vol. 2, p. 154.

17   The coverage of Clara's death in the *Denver Republican*, October 27, 1885, says that her "brother Jack Smith of Georgetown, an aged colored man, hastened to her side...." Again, it seems as though familial connections are assumed by white reporters where none existed. The 1870 census also provides no help, identifying a mulatto Jackson Smith, laborer, aged 52, Kentucky-born. But there is also a Jackson Smith, aged 40, also a laborer and also Kentucky-born, with no race identified.

18   Young, Frank, *Echoes from Arcadia* (Denver, [Laning Brothers], 1903) 96.

19   Clear Creek County Grantor-Grantee Book 2, p. 223. There are also references to a Charles Poynter around the same time; he and Henry sold two lots in Eureka Gulch for $10 in September, 1865, according to Gilpin County Record Book 21, p. 81. In a record of money orders issues from the Mountain City Post Office during this

period, compiled by the Foothills Genealogical Society, there is a transaction between Charles and a Thomas Poynter and Henry. And Bruyn, in a letter to Fisk University seeking help on black pioneers, says that Jack Smith and *James* Poynter were the relatives who came back with Clara in 1866. Bruyn papers, DPL/WHC.

20 Bancroft, 258, 262, Bancroft's account also clearly parallels that of Donald C. Kemp in his *Colorado's Little Kingdom* (p. 63), written some years earlier. The additional details supplied by Bancroft may well have been merely products of her own perfervid imagination.

21 Gilpin County Record Book 9, p. 187.

22 Ruby died of smallpox in Black Hawk in 1885, as did the couple's son, George Jr.

23 Gilpin County Record Book 44, p. 142.

24 Randall Clippings, Vol. 1, p. 37-38.

25 *Rocky Mountain Herald*, Oct. 21, 1886.

26 *Denver Republican*, October 27, 1885.

27 Hafen, LeRoy R., *Colorado and Its People* (New York: Lewis Historical Publishing Co., 1948) 565.

28 *Register*, Sept. 25, 1868.

29 Hall, 484.

30 Founded in 1833, the college is centered around Tappan Square, named for the four-story Tappan Hall, built in 1835. Bigglestone, William R., *Oberlin: From War to Jubilee, 1866-1883* (Oberlin: Grady Publishing Co., 1983) 17 ff.

Chapter 9

1 Or with the governor. Hill pronounced him "the most unpractical man I ever knew." Letter to his wife, Alice, quoted in Smith, *The Birth of Colorado* 201.

2 Smith, *The Birth of Colorado* 202. The house still stands at the mouth of Chase Gulch in Black Hawk.

3 Burrell, 453.

4 Kemp, 122.

5 Pearce's home across from Hill's in Chase Gulch also still stands. After moving to Denver with the relocation of the smelting works in 1878, Pearce built a mansion on Sherman Street; he retired from the smelting business in 1901.

6 Hill also was, throughout much of this period, the owner of the *Denver Republican*. One can speculate whether the large amount of coverage the paper gave Clara during the 1880's was due to the owner's fond memories of her from his days in Black Hawk.

7 Kemp, 85.

8 State of Colorado, *General Laws*, Fourth Session, p. 122-3.

9 *The Charter and Ordinances of the City of Central*, p. 101-2.

10 King, William M., "Black Children, White Law," *Essays in Colorado History*, No. 3, 1984, 71-2.

11 *Tri-Weekly Miners Register*, April 26, 1865.

12   *Daily Central City Register*, Sept. 15, 1869.

13   Ford's role is discussed at length, if somewhat fancifully, in Parkhill, *Mister Barney Ford: A Portrait in Bistre.*

14   *Daily Central City Register*, March 19, 20, 1868.

15   Gilpin County Register of Warrants, 1866-1876.

16   Gilpin County Treasurer's Warrant Register.

17   Thomson *Diary*, May 18, 1872.

18   *Register*, June 3, 1870.

19   Gilpin County Record Book 45, p. 255.

20   *Register*, July 17, 1868. George K. Sabin was the father of Florence Sabin, public health pioneer, whose bust is included among those found in the rotunda of the United States Capitol.

21   *Register*, Feb. 19, 1868.

22   *Register*, Feb. 18, 1868.

23   *Register*, Feb. 20, 1868.

24   *Register*, Feb. 22, 1868.

25   *Register*, May 24, 1868.

26   *Register*, Feb. 19, 1870. The case took on an even stranger aspect the following day. "The colored people of Central, having reason to believe that a certain physician who had threatened as much, would attempt to dig up the body of the criminal Smith, for dissection, arranged a guard the first half of which was to go on at 7 o'clock. When, at the hour, they approached the grave they found a party already digging, who fired on them, compelling them to leave. A policeman believed he saw the dissection going on some two hours later. He had proposed to guard against such a thing but they stole a march on him." *Register*, Feb. 20, 1870. While it is tempting to assign some of the blame for this outrage to Smith's race, the fact is that executed criminals were considered "fair game" for the body snatchers. Still, the willingness of the black citizens to protect the body from the despoiling indicates a strong sense of community, and may be another evidence of their belief in Smith's innocence—or at least his unfair treatment. Still later, when a ghost was seen in Eureka Gulch, some recalled "the hanging of negro George on the mountain top near by, for his murderous work in Chase gulch...." *Register*, Jan. 19, 1874.

27   *Register*, July 28, 1869.

28   *Register*, Jan. 28, 1878.

29   *Register*, Jan. 29, 1878.

30   *Register*, Jan 31, 1878.

31   *Register*, Feb. 22, 1878.

32   *Register*, March 20, 1878.

33   *Register,* April 24, 1878.

34   *Register*, Dec. 29, 1870.

35   Burrell, 321.

36   *Georgetown Miner*, July 30, 1869.

37   Burrell, 239.

38   Fish remarried, apparently unhappily; his new wife, Jane, was later "arrested and acquitted of the charge of poisoning her husband...." *Register-Call*, June 14, 1901.

39   An excellent treatment of Hamill's career is in Christine Bradley's *William A. Hamill, the Gentleman from Clear Creek*. His primary partner in mining property was Jerome Chaffee, later one of Colorado's first two U.S. senators. Hamill's beautifully restored home and compound is now the centerpiece of the restoration efforts conducted by Historic Georgetown, Inc.

40   Peter McFarlane's daughter-in-law, Ida Kruse McFarlane, was the guiding light behind the reopening of the Opera House in 1932, along with Anne Evans, the daughter of another prominent pioneer, Colorado's second territorial governor, John Evans. The history of the opera has been told in numerous books and articles; the best information on McFarlane is H. William Axford's *Gilpin County Gold*.

41   Several photographs in the collection of the Denver Public Library—X2868, for example—show the tiny building next to the Opera House but mistakenly identify it as "a wood frame house." Adding to the confusion, a lengthy article on the church's history, published more than forty years later, stated that the building had originally been a livery stable, modified for ecclesiastical use by Will and Peter McFarlane; the author probably remembered the stables that were relocated for the construction of the Opera House next door. *Register*, Aug. 4, 1916.

42   *Rocky Mountain Sunday School Casket*, Dec. 1865.

43   *Denver Republican*, March 4, 1882.

44   Granruth, *Mining Gold to Mining Wallets*, 94. Burrell, 240, wrote that the "total cost must have exceeded $20,000."

45   *Register*, July 17, 1868.

46   *Register,* April 18, 1872.

47   *Rocky Mountain News*, April 19, 1872.

48   Hollenback, Frank, *Central City and Black Hawk* (Denver: Sage Books, 1960) 63.

49   *Register*, Jan. 25, 1873.

50   *Register*, Oct. 4, 1873.

51   Axford, 60.

52   Axford, 61.

53   Bruyn papers, WHC/DPL.

54   *Rocky Mountain News* May 21, 1968; June 13, 1968. Pearce and Pfaff seem to suggest a reason of gratitude, writing that Lee "then rented the house to Thomas Hale Potter, who had shown him how to invest his money." *Guide to Historic Central City & Black Hawk*, p. 34.

55   To be fair, there is some language that suggests that the building was erected for the purpose of renting it out. The *Register-Call* reported during construction that "[t]he residence of Major Hal Sayr on High street, and that being erected by Mr. Jerry Lee, west of County Road, on High street, will soon receive the attention of the brick masons. The foundation walls are already completed." The notation that the house was merely "being erected" by Lee could indicate it was not originally intended for his personal residence. *Register-Call*, Oct. 21, 1881.

Notes

Chapter 10

1 *Register*, April 16, 1867.
2 *Register*, April 25, 1867.
3 Athearn, Robert G., *In Search of Canaan: Black Migration to Kansas, 1879-80* (Lawrence: Regents Press of Kansas, 1978) 76.
4 *Register*, Jan. 4, 1878.
5 *Register*, Sept. 28, 1871.
6 *Register*, Sept. 4, 1874.
7 Athearn, 91.
8 Quoted in *Topeka Commonwealth*, May 8, 1879.
9 *Wyandotte Gazette*, August 29, 1879.
10 *Topeka Commonwealth*, May 1, 1879.
11 Katz, William Loren, *The Black West* (New York: Simon & Schuster, 1996) 175.
12 *Topeka Commonwealth*, May 8, 1879.
13 *Topeka Commonwealth*, May 8, 1879.
14 Quoted in Cutler, *History of the State of Kansas,* Part 34.
15 Katz, 175.
16 Athearn, 161.
17 Denver *Daily Tribune*, May 10, 1879.
18 Denver *Daily Tribune*, May 10, 1879.
19 Quoted in Athearn, 162.
20 Denver *Daily Tribune*, May 11, 1879.
21 Athearn, 162.
22 Athearn, 162.
23 *New York Times*, May 10, 1879.
24 Quoted in *Topeka Commonwealth*, August 7, 1879.
25 Stiff, 21.
26 *Denver Republican*, March 17, 1890.
27 Athearn, 162.
28 *Weekly Register-Call*, September 26, 1879.
29 Athearn, 163-4.
30 *Topeka Commonwealth*, July 17, 1879.
31 *Kansas Methodist*, October, 1879.
32 Burrell, 443. Though the sketch was published in 1880, it may well have been written prior to Aunt Clara's return from Kansas in September, 1879.
33 Hornbein, Marjorie, *Temple Emanuel of Denver: a centennial history.* (Denver: A.B. Hirschfeld Press, 1974)
34 *Denver Republican*, October 27, 1885.
35 Treasurer's Warrant Register, July 30, 1873.

Chapter 11

1 *Denver Republican*, February 18, 1882.
2 *Denver Republican*, February 18, 1882; March 7, 1884; October 27, 1885.
3 *Denver Republican*, March 7, 1884.
4 Several of Chever's early office buildings were destroyed for the Skyline Urban Renewal Project. *Rocky Mountain News*, October 11, 1969.
5 *Rocky Mountain News*, April 5, 1867.
6 *Denver Republican*, February 18, 1882.
7 *Denver Republican*, February 18, 1882.
8 Randall clippings, Vol. I, pp. 25-6.
9 Confusing the issue still further, a *Register-Call* blurb of July 9, 1880, mentions that Clara Brown, "of this city," attended a camp-meeting in Arvada, which would seem to indicate that the reporter, at least, thought she still resided in Central City. There is some indication that Clara was in Central City through December.
10 Gilpin County Record Book 46, p. 379-381; Feb. 15, 1870.
11 *Register-Call*, March 25, 1881.
12 Gilpin County Record Book 82, p. 526; July 7, 1882.
13 *Denver Republican*, February 18, 1882.
14 *Denver Republican*, February 18, 1882.
15 Quoted in *Denver Republican*, March 4, 1882.
16 *Denver Republican*, April 18, 1882.
17 *Denver Republican,* June 26, 1885.
18 *Denver Republican*, October 27, 1885.
19 *Denver Republican*, February 18, 1882.
20 *Denver Republican*, February 18, 1882.
21 *Denver Republican*, April 18, 1882.
22 *Register-Call*, Feb. 25, 1882. The same paper also ran a brief mention of her return in the issue of April 14, 1882.
23 *Denver Republican*, April 18, 1882.
24 *Denver Republican*, October 27, 1885.
25 *Denver Republican*, June 26, 1885.

Chapter 12

1 GCPA papers, DPL/WHC.
2 *Register-Call*, Feb. 15, 1884. Clearly, this account differs in many particulars from that described in the letter, and later covered by the March 7, 1884 *Republican*. It may have been a second, entirely separate event. More likely, it was soon recognized by the organizers that Aunt Clara's renown and the respect in which she was held were so great that any fundraiser on her behalf would prove to be far too well attended to be held in Mr. Peck's property, and thus was moved to City Hall.
3 *Denver Republican*, March 7, 1884.
4 GCPA papers, DPL/WHC.

5   *Denver Republican*, January 26, 1881.
6   The Gilpin pioneer association had been organized in 1882, and began holding annual banquets thereafter. Interestingly, when word had reached A.G. Rhoads that there were plans to invite Aunt Clara to attend the 1884 reunion, he fired off a letter in mock outrage, wondering why he was not invited. GCPA papers, DPL/WHC.
7   *Register-Call*, Jan. 18, 1884.
8   *Register-Call*, Feb. 15, 1884.
9   *Denver Republican*, June 26, 1885.
10 *Denver Republican*, October 27, 1885.
11 *Rocky Mountain Herald*, October 21, 1886.
12 *Denver Republican*, September 27, 1885.
13 *Denver Republican*, June 26, 1885.
14 *Denver Republican*, October 23, 1885.
15 *Denver Republican*, October 27, 1885.
16 *Denver Republican*, October 27, 1885, as the next few references.
17 *Denver Republican*, October 30, 1885.

Chapter 13

1   Beardsley, 358-9.
2   *Kansas Farmer*, August 20, 1879.
3   *Rocky Mountain Herald*, October 21, 1886. Lest readers think this exaggerated, Jesse Randall wrote in his profile of Jeremiah Lee that "he thought nothing of walking from Central City to Georgetown and return, once or twice a week." That's an even greater distance, and over extremely rugged terrain.
4   *Denver Republican*, October 27, 1885.
5   Thomson, *Diary*, entry of May 18, 1872.
6   *Denver Republican*, June 26, 1885.
7   Young, 96.
8   *Denver Republican*, June 26, 1885.
9   Thomson, *Diary*, entry of May 18, 1872.
10 *Denver Republican*, June 26, 1885.
11 Thomson, *Diary*, entry of May 18, 1872.
12 *Denver Republican*, September 27, 1885.
13 *Weekly Register-Call*, September 29, 1885.
14 Bruyn papers, DPL/WHC.
15 Thomson, *Diary*, entry of May 18, 1872.
16 *Denver Republican*, February 18, 1882.
17 Quoted in *Denver Republican*, March 4, 1882.
18 GCPA papers, DPL/WHC.
19 *Denver Republican*, June 26, 1885.
20 *Denver Republican*, June 26, 1885.
21 Bruyn papers, DPL/WHC.

22   *Denver Republican*, June 26, 1885.

23   Hall, 483.

24   Thomson, *Diary*, entry of May 18, 1872.

25   *Denver Republican*, June 26, 1885.

26   Bruyn papers, DPL/WHC.

27   *Denver Republican*, June 26, 1885.

28   *Register-Call*, Oct. 30, 1885.

29   The "Professional Directory" in the Nov. 15, 1866, *Daily Miner's Register*, listed "ORRIS KNAPP, Manufacturer and dealer in Saddlery, Lawrence St., Central City." Knapp also owned property as early as 1861 in the mining district that eventually became the city of Black Hawk. Enterprise Mining District Record Book C, p. 16, 56.

30   *The Glory that was Gold*, (Central City Opera House Association, 1992) 43. The hickory chairs were replaced by comfortable, modern theatre-style seating in 1999. A little history was lost, but comfort was greatly enhanced.

31   The first two books in the series entitled "Chronicles of the Golden Frontier," written by Gilbert Morris and J. Landon Ferguson, published by Crossway Books, both have Aunt Clara as a minor character.

32   *Washington Post*, January, 1998.

33   *Register-Call*, June 4, 1886.

34   *Register-Call*, June 14, 1890.

35   *Register-Call*, March 21, 1889.

36   *Register-Call*, April 16, 1889.

37   *Register-Call*, Aug. 30, 1895.

38   *Register-Call*, Sept. 6, 1895.

39   *Register-Call*, Nov. 2, 1894.

40   *Register-Call*, Feb. 22, 1907.

41   *Georgetown Miner*, December 29, 1870.

42   *Register*, Dec. 18, 1870.

43   *Register*, Dec 29, 1870.

44   *Register-Call*, Aug. 31, 1883.

45   *Register-Call*, June 4, 1889.

46   *Register-Call*, June 5, 1889.

47   *Register-Call*, May 29, 1891.

48   Billy Hamilton also took the only known picture of Jennie. Noted earlier as a "trickster," he was probably also responsible for a "doctored" version of this photograph that showed the head of Fred Bauer, Black Hawk's disgraced marshal (he skipped town after failing to turn over all the tax monies he collected), in the laundry basket on Jennie's hip.

49   *Rocky Mountain News*, April 14, 1869.

50   Bruyn, 191.

51   Judging from Harriet Mason's headstone. The interment record, however, shows a date of May 19, 1903.

52 Block 9, Lots 24 & 25. Gilpin County Record Book 60, p. 603.

53 If Harriet Mason was one of the emigrants Clara brought back from Kentucky after the Civil War, it would also help explain the naming of that state, rather than Virginia, as Clara's birthplace on her new gravestone; Harriet Mason had probably heard Clara talk about her old home many times, and not realized that she was born and lived her first few years in Virginia.

Selected Bibliography

Adriance, Fr. Jacob; *Diary*, Vol. 4 & 5.

Arps, Louisa Ward, "The Gravity Tram of Gilpin County", *Denver Westerners' Roundup* Vol. XXV No. 1 (January 1969) 3-17.

Athearn, Robert G., *In Search of Canaan: Black Migration to Kansas, 1879-80.* Lawrence: Regents Press of Kansas, 1978.

Athearn, Robert G., *Westward the Briton.* New York: Charles Scribner's Sons, 1953.

Atkins, Joseph, *Human Relations in Colorado.* Denver: Colorado State Department of Education, 1961.

Axford, H. William, *Gilpin County Gold: Peter McFarlane, 1848-1929, Mining Entrepreneur in Central City, Colorado.* Chicago: Swallow Press, 1976.

Bancroft, Caroline, *Gulch of Gold.* Boulder: Johnson Publishing Co., 1958.

Barney, Libeus, *Letters of the Pikes Peak Gold Rush.* San Jose: Talisman Press, 1959.

Beardsley, Isaac Haight, *Echoes From Peak and Plain: or, Tales of life, war, travel and Colorado Methodism.* Cincinnati: Curtis & Jennings, 1898.

Belden, Tonya, *The Book of African-American Women: 150 Crusaders, Creators, and Uplifters.* Adams Media Corporation, 1996.

Bender, Norman J., "Crusade of the Blue Banner in Colorado," *Colorado Magazine,* Vol. 47, No. 2 (Spring 1970), 91-118.

Bigglestone, William E., *Oberlin: From War to Jubilee, 1866-1883.* Oberlin: Grady Publishing Co., 1983.

Bigglestone, William E., "Oberlin College and the Negro Student, 1865-1940," *The Journal of Negro History* 56 (July, 1971) 198-219.

Bluemel, Elinor, *Florence Sabin: Colorado Woman of the Century.* Boulder: University of Colorado Press, 1959.

Bowles, Samuel, *Across the Continent: A Summer's Journey to the Rocky Mountains, the Mormons, and the Pacific States, with Speaker Colfax.* Springfield, Mass.: Samuel Bowles & Company, 1865.

Bradley, Christine, *William A. Hamill.* [Ft. Collins]: Colorado State University Cooperative Extension Service, [n.d.].

Breck, Allen duPont, *The Centennial History of the Jews of Colorado.* Denver: Hirschfeld Press, 1960.

Burrell, James, "History of Gilpin County," in *History of Clear Creek and Boulder Valleys, Colorado.* Chicago: O.L. Baskin & Co., 1880.

Bruyn, Kathleen, *"Aunt" Clara Brown: Story of a Black Pioneer.* Boulder: Pruett, 1970.

Bruyn, Kathleen, "Matthias Klaiber, Physician and Minister," *Colorado Magazine* XXIII, 3 (July 1956) 197-208.

Bibliography

Carter, Louis J., *Yesterday Was Another Day*. Black Hawk: One Stop Printing, [n.d.].

Clearfield, Elaine Abrams, *Our Colorado Immortals in Stained Glass*. [Denver]: Mountain Bell, 1986.

Cimprich, John, "Slave Behavior During the Federal Occupation of Tennessee, 1862-1865," *The Historian* 44 (May, 1982) 335-46.

Cochran, Alice Cowan, *Miners, merchants and missionaries: the roles of missionaries and pioneer churches in the Colorado gold rush and its aftermath, 1858-1870.* Metuchen, N.J.: Scarecrow Press, 1980.

Coleman, J. Winston, Jr., *Slavery Times in Kentucky*. Chapel Hill: University of North Carolina Press, 1940.

Cox, Terry, *Inside the Mountains: A History of Mining Around Central City, Colorado.* Boulder: Pruett, 1989

Cushman, Samuel and J.P. Waterman, *The Gold Mines of Gilpin County, Colorado.* Central City: Register Steam Printing House, 1876.

Davis, Herman S., ed., *Reminiscences of General William Larimer...* Lancaster, Pa.: New Era Printing Co., 1918.

Davis, Sylvester, "Diary of Sylvester Davis," *New Mexico Historical Review*, VI, No. 4 (October 1931) 383-416.

Digerness, David S., *The Mineral Belt, Vol. III: Georgetown - Mining - Colorado Central Railroad.* Silverton, Colo.: Sundance Publications, 1982.

Dorset, Phyllis Flanders, *The New Eldorado: The Story of Colorado's Gold and Silver Rushes*. New York: Macmillan, 1970.

Dunn, William R., "*I Stand by Sand Creek:*" *A Defense of Colonel John M. Chivington.* Ft. Collins: Old Army Press, 1985.

Fell, James E., Jr., *Ores to Metals: The Rocky Mountain Smelting Industry*. Lincoln: The University of Nebraska, 1979.

Ferrell, Mallory Hope, *The Gilpin Gold Tram*. Boulder: Pruett, 1970.

Fiester, Mark, *Look for Me in Heaven: the Life of John Lewis Dyer.* Boulder: Pruett, 1980.

Finley, Alex C., *History of Russellville and Logan County.* Frankfort: University of Kentucky.

Fitzgerald, Ruth Coder, *A Different Story: A Black History of Fredericksburg, Stafford, and Spotsylvania, Virginia.* [Greensboro, N.C.]: Unicorn, 1979.

Flanagan, Mike, *Out West*. New York: Abrams, 1987.

Glazer, Sidney, ed., "A Michigan Correspondent in Colorado, 1878," *Colorado Magazine,* Vol. 37 No. 3 (July 1960) 207-218.

Goode, Rev. William H., *Outposts of Zion, with Limnings of Mission Life*. Cincinnati: Poe & Hitchcock, 1864.

Goodykoontz, Colin B., "Colorado as Seen by a Home Missionary, 1863-1868," *Colorado Magazine*, XII, No. 2 (March 1935).

Granruth, Alan, *A Guide to Downtown Central City, Colorado.* Central City: 1989.

Granruth, Alan, *The Little Kingdom of Gilpin: Gilpin County, Colorado.* [Central City]: Gilpin Historical Society, 2000.

134

Bibliography

Granruth, Alan, *Mining Gold to Mining Wallets: Central City, Colorado, 1859-1999*. [Central City: Gilpin Historical Society], 1999.

Griswold, Don and Jean, *Colorado's Century of "Cities."* Denver: Smith-Brooks Printing Co., 1958.

Guerin, Elsa Jane, *Mountain Charley: or the Adventures of Mrs. E.J. Guerin, who was thirteen years in male attire*. Norman: University of Oklahoma Press, 1968.

Hafen, LeRoy R., *Colorado and Its People: A Narrative and Topical History of the Centennial State*. New York: Lewis Historical Publishing Co., 1948.

Hafen, LeRoy R., ed., *Colorado Gold Rush: Contemporary Letters and Reports 1858-1859*. Philadelphia: Porcupine Press, 1974.

Hafen, LeRoy R., "The Last Years of James P. Beckwourth," *Colorado Magazine* 4 (August, 1928) 137 ff.

Hafen, LeRoy R., ed. *Overland Routes to the Gold Fields, 1859, from contemporary diaries*. Philadelphia: Porcupine Press, 1974.

Hafen, LeRoy R., ed., *Pike's Peak Gold Rush Guidebooks of 1859 by Luke Tierney, William B. Parsons, and summaries of the other fifteen*. Philadelphia: Porcupine Press, 1974.

Hafen, LeRoy R., "Steps to Statehood in Colorado," *Colorado Magazine*, III, No. 3 (Aug. 1926).

Hafen, LeRoy R., and Ann W. Hafen, eds., *Reports from Colorado: The Wildman Letters 1859-1865 with other related letters and newspaper reports, 1859*. Glendale, Ca.: The Arthur H. Clark Co., 1961.

Halaas, David Fridtjof, *Boom Town Newspapers: Journalism on the Rocky Mountain Mining Frontier, 1859-1881*. Albuquerque, N.M.: University of New Mexico Press, 1981.

Hall, Frank, *History of the State of Colorado*. Chicago: Blakely Printing Company, 1889.

Hanington, C.H., "Early Days of Central City," *Colorado Magazine,* Vol. XIX No. 1 (Jan. 1942) 3-14.

Harvey, James Rose, *Negroes in Colorado*. (Master's Thesis) [Denver]: University of Denver, 1941.

Henderson, Charles W., *Mining in Colorado: A History of Discovery, Development and Production*, Professional Paper No. 138. Washington: U.S. Geological Survey, 1926.

Hill, Alice Polk, *Tales of the Colorado Pioneers*. Denver: Pierson & Gardner, 1884.

Hollenback, Frank R., *Central City and Black Hawk, Colorado, Then and Now.* Denver: Sage Books: 1960.

Hollister, Ovando J., *The Mines of Colorado.* Springfield, Mass.: Samuel Bowles & Company, 1867.

Hornbein, Marjorie, *Temple Emanuel of Denver: a centennial history*. Denver: A.B. Hirschfeld Press, 1974.

Jones, Linda, "Aunt Clara Brown, The Beloved Pioneer of Colorado," *Colorado Gambler*, (Feb. 16, 1995) 14, 19.

Bibliography

Jones, William H., *The History of Catholic Education in the State of Colorado.* Washington, D.C.: The Catholic University of America Press, 1955.

Katz, William Loren, *The Black West: a Documentary and Pictorial History of the African American Role in the Westward Expansion of the United States.* New York: Simon & Schuster, 1996.

Kelsey, Harry E., *Frontier Capitalist: The Life of John Evans.* Denver: State Historical Society of Colorado, 1969.

Kemp, Donald C., *Colorado's Little Kingdom.* Golden: Sage Books, 1949.

King, Joseph E., *A Mine to Make a Mine: Financing the Colorado Mining Industry, 1859-1902.* College Station, Texas: Texas A&M University Press, 1977.

King, William M., "Black Children, White Law: Black Efforts to Secure Public Education in Central City, Colorado, 1864-1869," *Essays in Colorado History* No. 3 (1984) 55-79.

Kolchin, Peter, *American Slavery, 1619-1877.* New York: Hill & Wang, 1993.

Lanza, Ruth Willett, "Aunt Clara Brown, The Black Angel of Central City," *True West* (April, 1991) 38-43.

Leach, Richard R., "Lewis N. Tappan," *The Trail*, IV (Dec. 1911) 19-22.

Leonard, Stephen J., "John Nicolay in Colorado: A Summer Sojourn and the 1863 Ute Treaty," *Essays in Colorado History*, Number 11 (1990).

Leonard, Stephen J. and Thomas Noel, *Denver: Mining Camp to Metropolis.* Niwot: University Press of Colorado, 1990.

Leonard, Stephen J., *Lynching in Colorado, 1859-1919.* Boulder: University Press of Colorado, 2002.

Leyendecker, Liston Edgington, *Bela Stevens Buell: Central City Entrepreneur (1836-1918).* (Doctoral Dissertation) Denver: University of Denver, 1966.

Leyendecker, Liston Edgington, *Robert L. Martin: Colorado Mining Man (1842-1918).* (Master's Thesis) Denver: University of Denver, 1961.

Leyendecker, Liston E., *Washington Hall: Gilpin County's Oldest Courthouse.* [Ft. Collins]: Colorado State University Cooperative Extension Service, [n.d.].

Lingenfelter, Richard E., *The Hardrock Miners: A History of the Mining Labor Movement in the American West, 1863-1893.* Berkeley: University of California, 1974.

Lowery, Linda, *One More Valley, One More Hill: The Story of Aunt Clara Brown.* New York: Random House, 2002.

Mallory, Samuel, "Overland to Pikes Peak with a Quartz Mill," *Colorado Magazine,* VIII, No. 3 (May 1931) 108-115.

Marshall, Thomas Maitland, *Early Records of Gilpin County, Colorado, 1859-1861.* Boulder: University of Colorado, 1920.

Metcalf, Kenneth, *Beginnings of Methodism in Colorado.* (Doctoral Dissertation) [Denver]: Iliff School of Theology, 1948.

Monahan, Doris, *Destination: Denver City.* Athens, Ohio: Swallow Press, 1985.

Morris, Gilbert & J. Landon Ferguson, *Unseen Riches.* Wheaton, Ill.: Crossway Books, 1999.

Morris, Gilbert & J. Landon Ferguson, *Above the Clouds*. Wheaton, Ill.: Crossway Books, 1999.

Morse, Charles W., "Colorado in '65 was no place for rest," *Denver Westerners Monthly Roundup*, Vol. XVI, No. 5 (May, 1960) 5-15.

Murphy, Richard W., *The Civil War: The Nation Reunited*. Alexandria, Va.: Time Life Books, 1987.

Noel, Thomas J. with Stephen J. Leonard and Kevin E. Rucker, *Colorado Givers: A History of Philanthropic Heroes*. Niwot, Colo.: University Press of Colorado, 1998.

Noel, Thomas (ed.), *The Glory That Was Gold.* [Denver]: Central City Opera House Association, 1992.

Painter, Nell Irvin, *Exodusters: Black Migration to Kansas after Reconstruction*. New York: Knopf, 1976.

Parkhill, Forbes, *Mister Barney Ford: A Portrait in Bistre*. Denver: Sage Books, 1963.

Paul, Rodman Wilson, *Mining Frontiers of the Far West, 1848-1880*. New York: Holt, Rinehart and Winston, 1963.

Pearce, Sarah J. & Christine Pfaff, *Guide to Historic Central City & Black Hawk*. Evergreen, Colo: Cordillera Press, 1987.

Perkin, Robert L., *The First Hundred Years: An Informal History of Denver and the Rocky Mountain News*. Garden City, N.Y.: Doubleday, 1959.

Perrigo, Lynn Irwin, ed., "H.J. Hawley's Diary, Russell Gulch in 1860," *Colorado Magazine,* Vol. XXX, No. 2, 133-149.

Perrigo, Lynn Irwin, "Law and Order in Early Colorado Mining Camps," *The Mississippi Valley Historical Review,* Vol. XXVIII, No. 1 (June 1941) 41-62.

Perrigo, Lynn Irwin, *A Social History of Central City, Colorado, 1859-1900.* (Doctoral dissertation) [Boulder]: University of Colorado, 1934.

Perrigo, Lynn Irwin, *The Little Kingdom: a Record Chiefly of Central City in the Early Days*. Boulder: 1934.

Peterson, Richard H., *The Bonanza Kings: The Social Origins and Business Behavior of Western Mining Entrepreneurs, 1870-1900*. Norman: University of Oklahoma Press, 1991.

Reyburn, Marjorie L, "James Thomson in Central City," *University of Colorado Studies*, Vol. 1, No. 2 (June 1940), 183-203.

Robinson, Cedric J., *Black Movements in America*. New York: Routledge, 1997.

Rogers, James Grafton, *The Rush to the Rockies*. Denver: State Historical Society of Colorado, 1957.

Rogers, James Grafton, *My Rocky Mountain Valley*. Boulder: Pruett, 1968.

Sayre, Hal, "Early Central City Theatricals and Other Reminiscences," *Colorado Magazine,* VI, No. 1 (Jan. 1929).

Smith, Duane A., *The Birth of Colorado: A Civil War Perspective*. Norman: University of Oklahoma Press, 1989.

Smith, Duane A., "Colorado's Urban-Mining Safety Valve," *Colorado Magazine*, Vol. XLVIII, 4 (1971) 299-318.

Bibliography

Smith, Duane A., *Mining America: The Industry and the Environment, 1800-1980*. Lawrence: University Press of Kansas, 1987.

Smith, Duane A., "My Profit, Your Land: Colorado Mining and the Environment, 1858-1900," in Smith, Duane A., ed., *A Taste of the West*. Boulder: Pruett, 1983.

Smith, Duane A., "Pikes Peak Fifty-Niner: The Diary of E. A. Bowen, " *Colorado Magazine*, Vol. 47, No. 4 (Fall 1970) p. 269-311.

Smith, Duane A., *Rocky Mountain Mining Camps: The Urban Frontier*. Lincoln: University of Nebraska, 1974.

Smith, Duane A., *Rocky Mountain West: Colorado, Wyoming & Montana, 1859-1915*. Albuquerque: University of New Mexico, 1992.

Spence, Clark C., *British Investments and the American Mining Frontier, 1860-1901*. Ithaca, N.Y.: Cornell University Press, 1958.

Spencer, Emma Dill Russell, *Green Russell and Gold*. Austin: University of Texas, 1966.

Spring, Agnes Wright, *Colorado Charley*. Boulder: Pruett, 1968.

Stiff, Cary, "Barney Ford: From slavery to riches," *Denver Post, Empire Magazine*, Aug. 3, 1969 20-26.

Stratton, David H., "The Snake River Massacre of Chinese Miners, 1887," in Smith, Duane A. (ed.), *A Taste of the West*. Boulder: Pruett, 1983.

[Student, Annette L.], *Walk Through Historical Riverside Cemetery*. Denver: Fairmount Heritage Foundation, 2001.

Summering in Colorado. Denver: Richards & Co., 1874.

Sweeney, Elizabeth Ann, "The Catholic Church at Central City," *Colorado Magazine*, Vol. XVIII, No. 5 (Sept., 1941) 181-6.

Talmadge, Marian and Iris Gilmore, *Barney Ford, Black Baron*. New York: Dodd Mead & Co., 1973.

Taylor, Bayard, *Colorado: A Summer Trip* [1866]. Niwot, Colo.: University Press of Colorado, 1989.

Taylor, Quintard, *In search of the Racial Frontier: African Americans in the American West, 1528-1990*. New York: W.W. Norton, 1998.

Thomson, James, *Poems and Some Letters of James Thomson*, Anne Ridler, ed. London: Centaur Press, 1963.

Todd, Arthur Cecil, *The Cornish Miner in America*. Truro: D. Bradford Barton Ltd., 1967.

Trimble, Sara Ridley, ed., "Behind the Lines in Middle Tennessee, 1863-1865: The Journal of Bettie Ridley Blackmore," *Tennessee Historical Quarterly*, XII, (1953) 48-80.

Uchill, Ida Libert, *Pioneers, peddlers, and tsadikim*. Denver: Sage Books, 1957.

Unseld, Teresa S., *Portfolios: African-Americans of the Old West*. Palo Alto: Dale Seymour Publications, 1997.

U.S. Bureau of the Census, *Negro Population in the United States*, 1790-1915. Washington, D.C.: Government Printing Office, 1918.

Varnell, Jeanne, "The Society Mansion of an Ex-Slave," *Empire Magazine*, Nov. 30, 1969, 24-28.

Vickers, W.B., "History of Colorado," in *History of Clear Creek and Boulder Valleys,*

Colorado. Chicago: O. L. Baskin & Co, 1880.

Villard, Henry, *The Past and Present of the Pike's Peak Gold Regions.* Princeton: Princeton University Press, 1932.

Wallihan, S.S. & Co., *The Rocky Mountain Directory and Colorado Gazetteer for 1871.* Denver: S. S. Wallihan & Co., 1871.

West, Elliott, *The Contested Plains: Indians, Goldseekers and the Rush to Colorado.* Lawrence, Kansas, 1998.

West, Elliott, "Women of the Rocky Mountain West," in Smith, Duane A. (ed.), *A Taste of the West.* Boulder: Pruett, 1983.

Willard, James F., "Sidelights on the Pike's Peak Gold Rush, 1858-1859," *Colorado Magazine,* XII, No. 1 (Jan. 1935) 2-13.

Willison, George F., *Here They Dug the Gold.* New York: Brentano's, 1931.

Wilson, Elinor, *Jim Beckwourth: Black Mountain Man and War Chief of the Crows.* Norman: University of Oklahoma, 1972.

Winne, Peter, "Historical Gleanings," *The Trail*, Vol. VII, No. 3 (August, 1915) 5-17.

Wolle, Muriel Sibell, *Bonanza Trail.* Chicago: Swallow Press, 1953.

Wolle, Muriel Sibell, *Stampede to Timberline*, rev. ed. Chicago: Swallow Press, 1974,

Wolle, Muriel Sibell, *Timberline Tailings.* Chicago: Swallow Press, 1977.

Young, Francis Crissey, *Echoes from Arcadia: The Story of Central City, as told by one of "The Clan."* Denver: [Laning Brothers], 1903.

Zamonski, Stanley W. and Teddy Keller, *The Fifty-Niners.* Denver: Sage Books, 1961.

Index

Index

Index

Index

Index